Camping Cookbook

250 Ridiculously Easy Campfire Recipes for your family and friends

Conrad Weaver

© Copyright 2020 by Conrad Weaver - All rights reserved.

This document is geared towards providing exact and reliable information in regards to the topic and issue covered. The publication is sold with the idea that the publisher is not required to render accounting, officially permitted, or otherwise, qualified services. If advice is necessary, legal or professional, a practiced individual in the profession should be ordered.

- From a Declaration of Principles which was accepted and approved equally by a Committee of the American Bar Association and a Committee of Publishers and Associations.

In no way is it legal to reproduce, duplicate, or transmit any part of this document in either electronic means or in printed format. Recording of this publication is strictly prohibited and any storage of this document is not allowed unless with written permission from the publisher. All rights reserved.

The information provided herein is stated to be truthful and consistent, in that any liability, in terms of inattention or otherwise, by any usage or abuse of any policies, processes, or Instructions: contained within is the solitary and utter responsibility of the recipient reader. Under no circumstances will any legal responsibility or blame be held against the publisher for any reparation, damages, or monetary loss due to the information herein, either directly or indirectly.

Respective authors own all copyrights not held by the publisher.

The information herein is offered for informational purposes solely, and is universal as so. The presentation of the information is without contract or any type of guarantee assurance.

The trademarks that are used are without any consent, and the publication of the trademark is without permission or backing by the trademark owner. All trademarks and brands within this book are for clarifying purposes only and are the owned by the owners themselves, not affiliated with this document.

Table of Contents

Introduction 11

Chapter 1: Camping – An Introduction 13

    1.1. Food Prep and Safety 14

    1.2. Packing for Camping 14

    1.3. Gearing Up: What You Need 16

    1.4. What You Absolutely Need for Camping 17

    1.5. Taking Your Camping Up a Notch 19

    1.6. Camping Food Hacks 20

Chapter 2: Planning Your Meals 22

    2.1. Dutch Oven Cooking 23

    2.2. Packing for Your Trip 24

    2.3. Dutch Oven Size 26

    2.4. Packing Your Cool Box or Esky 27

    2.5. Packing Non-Perishable Foods 28

    2.6. Essential Food Items 29

    2.7. Salad Ingredients 31

    2.8. Tea, Coffee and Hot Chocolate 32

    2.9. Camping Cooking Utensils 32

Chapter 3: Camping Main Dishes 35

    3.1. Parmigiana Chicken 35

    3.2. Basil Chicken 36

    3.3. French Chicken 37

    3.4. Simple Chicken Thighs 38

    3.5. Favorite Honey Chicken 39

    3.6. Chicken Cacciatore 40

    3.7. Asian Chicken Breast 41

    3.8. Orange Ginger Wings 42

    3.9. Herbed Chicken 42

    3.10. Herby Chicken with Pesto 43

    3.11. Creamy Chicken in Gravy 45

    3.12. Chicken with Raisins and Rice 46

    3.13. Chicken Breasts Stuffed with Pesto 46

    3.14. Curried Chicken and Fruit 48

3.15. Wild Rice with Chicken ... 49

3.16. Sunny Chicken ... 50

3.17. Cranberry Chicken ... 51

3.18. Amish Filling ... 52

3.19. "Stir-Fry" Chicken and Broccoli ... 53

3.20. Cornish Game Hens with Bacon and New Potatoes ... 54

3.21. Mexican Supper-in-a-Crock ... 55

3.22. Arroz con Pollo ... 56

3.23. Tex-Mex Chicken Roll-ups ... 57

3.24. Italian Chicken Fajita Wraps ... 58

3.25. Turkey with Mushroom Sauce ... 60

3.26. King Turkey ... 61

3.27. Turkey Barbecue Makes ... 61

3.28. Creamy Turkey with Vegetables Dinner ... 63

3.29. Barbecued Turkey Cutlets (with a great variation) ... 64

3.30. Turkey Salad ... 64

3.31. Turkey Enchiladas ... 65

3.32. Mustard-Glazed Tomatoes ... 67

3.33. Campfire Chili ... 67

3.34. Shredded Baked Potatoes ... 68

3.35. Grilled Portobello Mushrooms ... 69

3.36. Greek Potatoes ... 69

3.37. Hobo Chicken and Vegetables ... 70

3.38. Grilled Salmon with Lemon ... 71

3.39. Hawaiian Style Pork Chops ... 72

3.40. Herb-Stuffed Grilled Fish ... 72

3.41. Margarita Pizza with Beer Crust ... 73

3.42. Pan-Fried Potatoes and Mushrooms ... 75

3.43. Slow-Cooked Pulled Pork ... 75

3.44. Caprese Chicken Skewers ... 76

3.45. Chicken Bacon Tootsies ... 77

3.46. Cajun Chicken Breast Sandwiches ... 77

3.47. Spit-Fire Chicken ... 78

3.48. Turkey Pimento Burgers ... 78

3.49. Jerk Chicken Legs ... 80

3.50. Beer Chicken and Fingerling Potatoes ... 81

Chapter 4: Camping Breakfast Recipes ... 82

4.1. Muffin Tin Bacon N Eggs ... 82
4.2. Berry Pancakes ... 83
4.3. Granola Bread ... 84
4.4. Grilled Banana Oatmeal Pancakes ... 84
4.5. Eggs Benedict ... 85
4.6. Camp-Style Chocolate Pitas ... 86
4.7. Cinnamon French toast ... 87
4.8. Camp Granola ... 87
4.9. Granola Bars ... 88
4.10. Fruity Fiber Cookies ... 89
4.11. Mini Frittatas ... 90
4.12. Hot Multigrain Cereal ... 90
4.13. Breakfast Burritos ... 91
4.14. Overnight Cheese Casserole ... 92
4.15. Muffin Tin Bacon and Eggs ... 92
4.16. Berry Pancakes ... 93
4.17. Grilled Banana Oatmeal Pancakes ... 94
4.18. Eggs Benedict ... 95
4.19. Camp-Style Chocolate Pitas ... 95
4.20. Cinnamon French toast ... 96
4.21. Camp Granola ... 96
4.22. Granola Bars ... 97
4.23. Fruity Fiber Cookies ... 98
4.24. Mini Frittatas ... 99
4.25. Peanut Butter Banana Muffins ... 99
4.26. Hot Multigrain Cereal ... 100
4.27. Breakfast Burritos ... 100
4.28. Overnight Cheese Casserole ... 101
4.29. Potato Subs (Indian) ... 102
4.30. Fruit Mix ... 103
4.31. Peanut Butter Banana ... 103

Chapter 5: Camping Midday Meals ... 105

5.1. Ranch Chicken Roll Ups ... 105
5.2. Cheesy Macaroni ... 106
5.3. Dilled Bean and Tomato Salad ... 106
5.4. Tomato Pasta Soup ... 107
5.5. Bean Tacos ... 108

- 5.6. Huevos Rancheros ... 108
- 5.7. Grilled Ham and Cheese ... 109
- 5.8. Penne Pesto with Tuna ... 110
- 5.9. Scrambled Eggs and Rice ... 110
- 5.10. Salmon Sandwiches ... 111
- 5.11. Quesadillas ... 111

Chapter 6. BBQ & Campfire Recipes ... 113

- 6.1. Classic Hamburgers ... 113
- 6.2. Fast-Seared Steaks with French Beans ... 114
- 6.3. Thai Chilly Beef Burgers ... 115
- 6.4. Sugar & Spice Glazed Beef ... 116
- 6.5. Green Peppercorn Steaks ... 117
- 6.7. Butterflied Leg of Lamb with Broad Bean & Dill Yogurt ... 118
- 6.8. Aromatic Barbecued Lamb ... 119
- 6.10. Taverna-Style Lamb with Feta Salad ... 120
- 6.11. Minted Lamb Kebabs ... 121
- 6.12. Barbecued Pork ... 122
- 6.13. Pork Escalopes with Lemon & Capers ... 123
- 6.14. Sticky Gammon Steaks with Caramelized Onions ... 123
- 6.15. Chorizo & Quail's Egg Pizzas ... 124
- 6.16. Seared Pork Chops with Chilli Corn ... 126
- 6.17. Spit-Roasted Pork with Apple Butter ... 126
- 6.18. Chicken Satay Skewers ... 128
- 6.19. Lemon & Parsley Chicken Skewers ... 129
- 6.20. Tandoori Chicken Skewers with cucumber & cumin salad ... 130
- 6.21. Blackened Chicken Skewers ... 131
- 6.22. Chicken Burgers with Tomato Salsa ... 132
- 6.23. Chicken & Mozzarella Skewers ... 133
- 6.24. Herb-Marinated Spatchcock Chicken ... 133
- 6.25. Spit-Roasted Chicken with Saffron Mayonnaise ... 135
- 6.26. Chicken Fajitas ... 136
- 6.27. Thai Barbecued Chicken ... 138
- 6.28. Prawn & Bacon Skewers ... 139
- 6.29. Scallop & Chorizo Skewers ... 140
- 6.30. Quick Tuna Steaks with green salsa ... 140
- 6.31. Blackened Tuna with Mango Salsa ... 142
- 6.32. Swordfish Steaks with Basil & Pine Nut Oil ... 143

6.33. Olive & Citrus Salmon 144

6.34. Stuffed Salmon Fillets with Pancetta & Tomatoes 144

6.35. Mackerel with Citrus Fennel Salad 145

6.36. Mackerel Fillets with Pickled Beetroot 146

6.37. Chargrilled Sardines with mango & lime salsa 147

6.38. Salt & Pepper Tiger Prawns with Baby Corn & Mango Salsa 148

6.39. Prawns with Piri 149

6.40. Potato & Cheese Burgers 150

6.41. Cheddar Burgers with Cucumber Salsa 151

6.42. Mushroom, Couscous & Herb Sausages 152

6.43. Tomato, Pesto & Olive Pizzas 153

6.44. Double Cheese Margherita Pizza 155

6.45. Indian Spiced Sweet Potatoes 156

6.46. Quick & Easy Crispy Lamb Moroccan Rolls 157

6.47. Linguine with Shredded Ham & Eggs 158

6.48. Meatballs, Peas & Pasta 159

6.49. Pappardelle with Figs, Gorgonzola & Parma Ham 160

6.50. Cheesy Turkey & Cranberry Melt 160

6.51. Jamaican Spiced Salmon with Corn & Okra 161

6.52. Tuna Quesadilla with Salsa 162

6.53. Pesto & Salmon Pasta 163

6.54. Pasta Salad with Crab, Lime & Rocket 164

6.55. Prawn, Mango & Avocado Wrap 164

6.56. Griddled Greek-Style Sandwiches 165

6.57. Mediterranean Goats' Cheese Omelettes 166

6.58. Caramelized Onion & Cheese Crêpes 167

6.59. Sweetcorn Fritters with Sweet Chilli Dip 168

6.60. Lemon, Ricotta & Courgette Ribbon 169

6.61. Curried Cauliflower, Lentil & Rice 170

6.62. Big Mac 'N' Cheese 171

6.63. Green Cheese Pasta 172

6.64. Refried Bean Quesadilla 173

6.65. Orzo Risotto with Pancetta & Peas 174

Chapter 7: Camping Sides; Salads, Sauces & Snacks Recipes 175

7.1. Sardines on Rye 175

7.2. Spiced Mackerel Fillets 176

7.3. Eggs Florentine 177

7.4. Smoked Mackerel Pasta Salad ... 178
7.5. Seared Tuna with Bean & Rocket Salad ... 179
7.6. Herbed Lamb with Fig Salad ... 180
7.7. Cypriot Chicken & Haloumi Salad ... 181
7.8. Chickpea & Herb Salad ... 182
7.9. Orange & Avocado Salad ... 183
7.10. Ribboned Carrot Salad ... 184
7.11. Griddled Haloumi with Warm Couscous Salad ... 185
7.12. Egg, Basil & Cheese Salad with Cherry Tomatoes ... 186
7.13. Spicy Sweet Potato & Feta Salad ... 187
7.14. Real Guacamole with raw vegetables ... 187
7.15. Warm Courgette & Lime Salad ... 189
7.16. Garlic Bread ... 189
7.17. Devilled Mushrooms ... 190
7.18. Tabbouleh with Fruit & Nuts ... 191
7.19. Green Couscous with Spiced Fruit Sauce ... 192
7.20. Thai-dressed Tofu Rolls ... 193
7.21. Tortillas with chilly & aubergine yogurt ... 194
7.22. Bean & Pepper Burritos ... 195
7.23. Sweet Potato, Bacon & Thyme Cakes ... 196
7.25. Fresh Tomato Sauce ... 197
7.26. Chorizo Cherry Tomato Sauce ... 198
7.27. Sauce Vierge ... 198
7.28. Lemon & Vodka Sauce ... 199
7.29. Dill & Mustard ... 200
7.30. Sweet Stuff & Drinks Hot Barbecued ... 201
7.31. Fruit Salad Kebabs ... 202
7.32. Griddled Peaches with Passion Fruit ... 203
7.33. Creole Pineapple Wedges ... 203
7.34. Mini Strawberry Shortcakes ... 204
7.35. Tipsy Blueberry Pots & Mascarpone ... 205
7.36. Sweet & Sour Spiced ... 205
7.37. Passion Fruit Yogurt Fool ... 206
7.38. Figs with Yogurt & Honey ... 207
7.39. Lemon & Passion Fruit Whips ... 207
7.40. Stewed Rhubarb with Custard ... 208
7.41. Blueberry & Orange Eton Mess ... 208

7.42. Cinnamon & Raisin Pear Trifle ... 209

7.43. Chocolate & Banana Melts ... 210

7.44. Blueberry & Ginger Patties ... 210

7.45. S'mores ... 211

7.46. Choc Cinnamon ... 212

7.47. Quick Kiwifruit & Ginger Cheesecakes ... 213

7.48. Glossy Chocolate Sauce ... 213

7.49. Apple Sauce ... 214

7.50. Mulled Cranberry & Red Wine ... 214

7.51. Frothy Hot Toddy Chocolate Drink ... 215

7.52. Rusty Nail ... 216

7.53. Whisky MAC ... 216

7.54. Pimm's Cocktail ... 217

7.55. Beer Flatbreads with Cheese & Onions ... 217

7.56. Corn Flatbreads with Sweetcorn & Gruyère ... 219

7.57. Balsamic Braised Leeks & Peppers ... 220

7.58. Mustard & Thyme Sweet Potatoes ... 220

7.59. Fire-Baked New Potatoes with Green Dressing ... 221

7.60. Balsamic-Roasted Tomatoes ... 222

7.61. Roasted Red Onions ... 223

7.62. Panzanella Originating from Tuscany, Italy ... 223

7.63. Crushed Minted Peas ... 224

Chapter 8: Camping Vegetarian Main and Side Recipes ... 225

8.1. Easy Skillet Mexican Corn on the Cob ... 225

8.2. African Sweet Potato and Peanut Stew ... 226

8.3. Tuscan White Bean Skillet with Tomatoes, Mushroom, and Arti Chokes ... 227

8.4 Skillet Veggie Lasagna ... 228

8.5 Easy Migas Recipe ... 230

8.6. Garlic Parmesan Broccoli and Potatoes in Foil ... 230

8.7. Middle Eastern Spiced Camp Fire Chickpeas ... 231

8.8. One Pot Quinoa Cannellini Beans Skillet ... 233

8.9. Kung Pao White Beans Skillet ... 234

8.10. Banana & Peanut Butter Quesadillas ... 235

8.11. Overnight Oats ... 236

8.12. Porridge ... 236

8.13. Halloumi Skewers ... 237

8.14. Quesadillas ... 237

Chapter 9: Camping Foil Recipes 239

9.1. Camping Breakfast Burritos 239

9.2. Campfire S'mores Granola 240

9.3. Lumber Jack Break Fast for Camping (in a tin foil) 242

9.4. Campfire Orange Cinnamon Rolls 243

9.5. Camp Fire Apple Pie Packets 243

9.6. Campfire Tex Mix White Bean Chicken Foil Packets 244

9.7. BBQ Party Pack for Campers 245

9.8. Hobo Dinners 247

9.9. Campfire Paella Foil Packet 248

9.10. Campfire Philly Cheesesteak Sandwich 248

9.11. BBQ Chicken and Potato Foil Packet 249

9.12. Easy Pineapple Upside down Cake in Foil Packet 250

9.13. Camp Fire Food: Fruit & Sore Cones 251

Chapter 10: Camping Bread Recipes 252

10.1 Zesty Grilled Garlic Bread 252

10.2. Bread-On-A-Stick 253

10.3. Warm Wild Berry Jam 253

10.4. Corn Tortillas 254

10.5. Cheddar Biscuit 255

10.6. Skillet Bread 256

Chapter 11: Camping Sea Food Recipes 257

11.1. Lime-Drizzled Fish Tacos 257

11.2. Orange Bacon Salmon Skewers 258

11.3. Grilled Shrimp and Mushrooms 259

11.4. Ying and Yang Salmon 259

11.5. Tequila Jalapeño Scallops 260

11.6. Grilled Snapper 261

Conclusion 262

Introduction

No one can forget the joy of their first camping trip. With campfires, buttered marshmallows, and nature drive helping to eradicate memories of soggy sleeping bags, torrential rain, and numb toes, the passage of years seems to bring a nostalgic slant to the whole journey. There is no questioning the excitement of a camping trip from preparing and packing to picking a pitch, setting up camps, and preparing meals over an open fire.

Camping offers a rare place for the inner kid to connect, reigniting the creative spirit broken down by the daily grind. And children excel on a holiday's liberty and adventures where the daily schedule is thrown aside, and no one nags them about personal hygiene. It's also an extraordinary chance to give them a few little responsibilities, which the independence they will enjoy will richly award them.

If you're going to fully enjoy the moment of camping, it's best to leave the modern world as far as possible at home. Even if you're struggling to get a Wi-Fi link and scoop up work emails, or you cut short the campfire banter to go inside and see telly, it's rare to communicate with nature. Camping is always about bringing yourself away from real life's frenetic speed and taking trips back to basics. It's about having a discussion over dinner rather than lying on the lounge in silence; it's about informing your kids that nature can cope with mobile phones and tablets on the amusement front. And, of course, without spending at least a whole day inside having the rain pour down, it wouldn't be a genuine camping experience.

The recipes provided for this book take the theme of basic outside grilling up a notch to the classic grilled dish with simple variations. You will be trying to revamp your camp cooking style with just a little seasoning and excitement, and your campmates will praise you for it. Camping is a time for friends and family to rest and communicate while also hooking up with the natural world, so it should be easy to cook. A perfect way to get beautiful layers of taste without a lot of effort is to pop stuff on the grill, and the aroma of those creations wafting through the air only adds a unique kind of fragrance, especially over an open flame in the evening.

This Camping Cookbook is packed with delicious, simple recipes that lead you on all kinds of taste trips from the beaten grill track. We want to affiliate you with real cooking food below. It means no chairs and tables, just grilling straight-up over a campfire or barbecue.

So, get outside, get delicious, and get exciting this summer with your campfire creations.

Happy grilling!

Chapter 1: Camping – An Introduction

Camping is an open-air activity that involves overnight stays in a camp, such as a tent or a motor home, close to nature. Participants usually leave urban areas to explore more natural areas in favor of activities that give us a sense of satisfaction. Camping separates the night (or more) spent outdoors from day-tripping, picnicking, and other equally short-term social activities. To multiple people, camping invokes different definitions. It portrays a forest adventure for the explorer. Camping is an escape, a family holiday, and an affordable space for a parent. In the following line, its popularity is noted: camping is indeed one of the best holiday values you can find worldwide. It is less pricey than staying at a restaurant, and as much as you like, you can take your food and cook. You get some clean air; you can sit outside watching the sights and enjoying the scenery. It also benefits a hotel because you don't know who's there beside you while you are there because nobody speaks to one another. The guys closest door come over or wave as soon as you pull into a camping site  and ask if you need anything. It's social, more so. And everyone has the same interest in a camping site as you do: hiking. Camping is a form of outdoor leisure that is part sport and part lodging. From simple tenting, it has now grown to include caravans, motor vehicles, and luxury options.

At the beginning of the 20th century, camping as a recreation practice became famous among insiders. It gained popularity among other socioeconomic groups overage. Modern campers visit natural spaces protected by the public, such as national and state parks, nature reserves, and commercial campsites. Like Scouting, Camping is a crucial pillar of many youth groups worldwide that use it to promote both self-reliance and collaboration.

It could be the clean air, the woody fragrances, or the birds' movements, the rushing waters, the falls in the wind. Whatever it is, it is so supremely wonderful and fully mystical for food prepared and enjoyed outdoors. On a bonfire grill, you can flip a plain simple burger, and it will transform into the most succulent, most juicy, most chomp-worthy burger you have ever had. So now, we've chosen to take the marvelous basis of tasty to a whole different extreme with crave-worthy camp recipes that are going to get you lighting up all year long.

1.1. Food Prep and Safety

Of course, after feasting on food that's been poisoned, and there's nothing pleasant about becoming hospitalized. Not only does it spoil your trip, but it is going to be until you get to a physician unless you're back in the country.

1.2. Packing for Camping

Get a cool looking cooler for longer camping trips rather than insulated bags. Such fellows are much better at storing food cool and can promise that you will get endlessness out the of food you carry.

The easiest thing to do is put your raw meat in your own cooler. Fully, not only is it the best that should be the norm.

When you carry your rice, use leak-proof containers or mason jars.

If you've prepared anything else to bring on your trip, cool it and carry it cold to stop the formation of harmful bacteria.

To ensure that they stay cold and don't get infected, it is vital that you pack your food products appropriately. With something in mind, if you really need to pack your raw meats and other foods together for some occasion, pack your raw things on the bottom so that there is no chance of leaking tainted liquids onto other foods.

You're pleased with food that needs to be kept in the fridge after you have packed your fridge. Now move on to stuff in warmer temperatures that will keep healthy, such as:

- Peanuts and dried fruit
- Nut butters
- Dried fish and meats
- Dried meats, Fruit drinks
- Pasta, rice, noodles

Definitely pack a beef thermometer so that you can ensure the food is tender all the way through.

Internal Temperature Cooking Charts in the appendix.

DONENESS TEMPERATURE FOR MEAT, POULTRY AND FISH

INGREDIENT	STOP COOKING WHEN TEMPERATURE REACHES	FINAL SERVING TEMPERATURE
BEEF & LAMB		
Rare	115 - 120°F	120 - 125°F (after resting)
Medium-Rare	120 - 125°F	125 - 130°F (after resting)
Medium	130 - 135°F	135 - 140°F (after resting)
Medium-Well	140 - 145°F	145 - 150°F (after resting)
Well-Done	150 - 155°F	150 - 160°F (after resting)
PORK		
Medium	140 - 145°F	145 - 150°F (after resting)
Well-Done	150 - 155°F	155 - 160°F (after resting)
CHICKEN		
Whilte Meat	160°F	160°F
Dark Meat	175°F	175°F
FISH		
Rare	110°F (for tuna only)	110°F
Medium-Rare	125°F (for tuna or salmon)	125°F
Medium	140°F (for white-fleshed fish)	140°F

1.3. Gearing Up: What You Need

Take a look at every collection or portal for camping equipment, and you will be persuaded that you need to pay thousands to get the goods. There should be nothing farther from the facts. Of course, some products are suitable to spend extra on, but other things don't have to be leading brands or brand new. While camping, also, there are

levels of comfort. We'll start with the basics and later step up to the more luxurious items

1.4. What You Absolutely Need for Camping

Tent: If you are going to stay away from the elements and keep yourself safe during the nights, a tent is necessary. You may use tents. However, you want to make sure they are leak-proof.

A tent should be big enough to accommodate everyone in your group (you should use more than one tent, conversely), but not too big. With just heat energy, big tents are a hassle to put up and tough to warm. Bear in mind that almost all tents are marked with how many people will fit, so you would want a little extra room to manoeuvre if you are small to large.

Ground Tarp: There has to be nothing fancy about a tarp, and it should be used. Its primary function is to shield the tent's bottom from pointy bits and provide an external layer against cold and moisture. To stop rain streaming under it, keep the tarp hidden under the tent.

Claw hammer: A hammer will help you strike the poles in the tent and as you leave, pull out the stems.

Sleeping Bag: The sleeping bag doesn't seem to be a premium brand or super costly, but it should be valued for the weather you're going to sleep. Check for a marked package for the coldest temperature at which you are going to camp out.

Sleep Pad: Keep nice and cozy with a mattress or sleeping pad. Cold ground will wick away your body heat, and in the middle of the night, you will end up frozen. To prevent this common problem, lay down a foam pad or an air-filled mattress. It would help if you still lay out a blanket for nothing else, helping to cush you from the surface.

Lantern/Flashlight: away from streetlights, it gets very, very dim. While there is some light in many existing campsites, most places will be much darker than you used to. Have a lamp to comfort you in the night to make your way to the toilet or tents. Flashlights are a staple on a camping trip, but because it keeps your hands free, you'll find a headlamp much more useful. A lantern can even be hanged in a forest or by a hook in the shelter to cast hands-free lighting.

Insect Repellent: Don't eat yourself alive! The holiday season is a perfect camping period, and it's an excellent time for bugs as well. To avoid long nights of scratching, cover every visible skin.

Water bottles: It is important to bring fresh water on walks, so make sure that you have a way to take some with you. If you intend to drink from lakes and rivers, water bottles with built-in filters can be useful, but any bottle would do freshwater.

Bucket: For anything from rinsing rice to getting water in, a bucket may be used. It is a smart idea to have a bucket of water next to the flames, too.

Food and Water: Over the next chapter, we'll get deeper into this, but it's still a smart idea to have some food on your side. If you like to be a fancier, bring some grown-up adult drinks, such as beer and wine, with you.

Matches: Without even a box of matches, you cannot start a fire quickly, so don't forget either!

Tinfoil: Even though you don't have a pot to cook in, tinfoil can be used to seal food for grilling or even make another use container for heating leftover food.

Knife: All over the campground, a good knife is essential. From whittling points on your roasting sticks to slicing up the newly caught cod for dinner, you'll need it for everything.

Rope: It's one of the stuffs that comes in handy. Rope may be used to hang up a tarp, bind sticks together to make a tepee for girls, or make dry clothing and sleeping bags with a clothesline.

Duct Tape: Whether you're hiking or not, you can still take duct tape on you. It has hundreds of applications, including wound taping, leakage in the tent patching, and stuff staying together.

Toilet Paper: They don't break the leaves. Said Enough. If you do your operation in the bush, carry your toilet paper rolls and some bin bottles to catch the trash in.

Soap: If you're at a campsite, staying clean is a necessity. You'll be shocked by how easily your hands and noses become dirty.

1.5. Taking Your Camping Up a Notch

Not so impressive, at the superficial level, in camping? Here's all you'll need to get a little more outdoor activity.

Welcome Mat: Tents appear to accumulate dust and dirt, so a little mat will help hold the residue away outside of the entrance to scrub feet on. There's nothing unique you don't need: Carry the mat from home.

Saw: For a campfire, fallen branches and trees are not the perfect sizes, and a saw makes it much easier for them to be cut into manageable pieces. If you are comfortable cutting wood, you should carry an axe as well.

Extra tarp: It's nice to have an additional tarp to string up over your sitting area if you end up in the rain, so you don't have to waste the whole night in the tent.

Air Pump: Preparing to use an inflatable mattress or another object that is packed with air? A pump is infinitely better, but you can fill it with air from your mouth. In case your inflatables are leaking, don't forget to bring a repair kit, too.

Pots and Pans: Leave at home your favorite pots and pans. The first meal over an open fire would blacken them. You can use standard pans if you are using a camp stove. Otherwise, visit the thrift store and see any affordable pots you can use without thinking about coal.

Camp Stove: A camp stove can be useful to have around whether there is a fire prohibition. You don't have to wait for the fire to burn out, and it can be difficult for those who are not used to cooking over an open fire. Much like a gas stove, a camp stove operates, so it is pretty straightforward to use.

Everybody is going to have their must-have commodities without which they can't survive. These are luxury items, so if you have to transport anything to the campsite, consider this! If you don't need anything you're taking, there's no sense in creating five trips between the car and the nearby campsite.

You will become a professional at packing light and paring down the weight after the first few camping trips to make your task easy. All it takes to realize precisely what you need is a long hike of too much weight for you.

1.6. Camping Food Hacks

So, part of the fun of cooking is imaginative in the outdoor activities. If you're a frequent camper, then you've definitely had to make cutlery or utensils out of some very weird items at one time or another.

- Check out any of the following camp food hacks on your camping trip that you should try out:

20

- Instead of squeezing your bread with all the other things you carry with you camping, keep your bread in a big, clean tin can. On the web, open it and eat sandwiches with non-squished-bread. To bake the bread, any recipe you like will be used.

- Freeze your drinking water in large containers which you can place inside your refrigerator. They can keep the cold cooler and can use it for drinking water later on.

- Take packets of tortilla flour as an additive to bread. They take up less space than bread for some chip-like action with salsa, which can be used to make wraps, thin pizzas, and even to crisp up.

- Find a salsa! Salsa is so portable and will give a new layer of taste to your camping meals. It can be found in many forms, such as a shake, cold pasta sauce, tacos, hot dogs, and numerous alternatives.

- If you are camping for a day or two, it is okay to cook meats and veggies with the required salt and black pepper, but if you decide to try the recipes in this book, you may want to take some other spices with you. In Tic-Tac packets, the packing of limited amounts is the best way to keep the spices portable.

- Grab some of that easy-burning wood, bag it, and take it with you in a flash to launch campfires if you live somewhere where you can get birch bark.

- You may make a compact grill with an aluminium tray filled with hot coals with a rack built on top.

- When cooking burgers over a grill, place an ice cube on each burger and you can keep the interior of the burger from drying out.

Chapter 2: Planning Your Meals

In this chapter, we will discuss a proper and healthy way to Plan your meals on a camping trip.

The first step of preparing your meals on a camping trip is to decide how long you're going to be away and how many meals you're going to eat in the natural surroundings. Your trip may be scheduled for four days, but are you going to prepare three meals a day during the four-day trip? Knowing the number of meals, you're going to cook helps minimize needless things that will not be used. Throughout the journey, it will also make sure you have quite enough food for all.

Secondly, recognize for whom you will be cooking while on your journey. Usually, for each adult, you want to prepare 1 1/2 servings and 1/2 servings for each kid. It's best to prepare for a little more if your kids are big eaters. At any stage during the journey, are you going to have friends with you? Ensure that any visitors who might come and how long they will be with you are taken into consideration. Mainly if you are out in the center of nowhere, it is better to have too much than too little.

You need to also consider the events that will take place on your camping trip while preparing your meals. Are you just leaving the big city to relax with a trickling brook or a fire? Are you going to go rafting in white water or taking long hikes during the day? Realizing the routines and activity level of your campers will decide how hungry everyone will be between meals and at mealtime. If you and your party are more involved

throughout the trip rather than relaxing around a fire reading a novel, you will be more likely to prepare protein-packed meals and snacks.

Your next move is to write out a meal plan after determining how long you will be camping, which you will be preparing for on the trip, and how involved your campers will be. Look at each day that you are going to camp and decide which meals you need to prepare. Set out the recipes and ingredients you need every day. Take into account the time you arrive at camp on the first day. You may be tired, so look for a fast and easy meal that doesn't take a lot of time to prepare or cook. Think about breaking down the camp and packing up if you intend to leave early on your final day.

The night before, it might be nice to cook something convenient that does not take any baking, such as foil-wrapped breakfast sandwiches that you can quickly reheat.

2.1. Dutch Oven Cooking

As you can plan meals as though you were in your own house, Dutch oven cooking is a go-to for several campers, giving you the chance to cook any of your favorite meals while enjoying the great outdoors. Cooking with a Dutch oven must begin with the purchase of a Dutch oven first. They range in size, and up to an army of Boy Scouts can support a single camper. Dutch ovens are made of aluminum or cast iron, and cast iron is the better choice unless you are backpacking, which allows you to conserve weight. At almost any sports goods shop, you will find Dutch ovens and the prices are relatively decent.

Depending upon where you make your order, a 10-inch oven will cost between $25 and $50. The bigger the oven, the more costly it is going to be. One suggestion to bear in mind: steer clear of the inexpensive ovens as they can be nothing but a hassle and take you back to the store for the next purchase shortly. Before buying, carefully check the range for any cracks.

The diameter in inches determines the oven size. Typically, the scale of the oven is quickly seen and will be on the lid. A guide to help you decide which size fits best for you is below.

2.2. Packing for Your Trip

The packing starts now that you've got a schedule in motion. Space may be a big problem if you are backpacking, or you may be in a family car with four kids, their luggage, bicycles, toys, tents, and the backyard kiddie tub. Regardless of how

you get to camp, saving space where it is feasible is always beneficial. Try to schedule dishes that use some of the same ingredients. It makes it easier to pack fewer containers for you. To assist in packing, it is also useful to mix products in advance. For example, if you have a recipe that needs 4-dry ingredients and 2-wet ingredients, instead of packing 6-separate containers, put the dry supplies in one container and the wet food items in a second container. Being imaginative about the containers that you use can also help save space. Try using a tic-tac jar for spices, including black ground pepper, salt, cinnamon, cumin, etc. Chances are, you won't need more than a single spice tic-tac jar at a time, and it's far lighter than taking along the pepper container you've got at home in your

grocery list. For your liquids, reuse plastic soda bottles (20 oz or 32 oz bottles from a grocery store) or small bottles of water. They are much smaller than the original bin, and after using them, they are easy to carry, taking up even less capacity on your way back home.

Aluminum foil is always a great aid, especially if you plan to cook hobo bags or camp potatoes, as you can arrange everything in a foil cooking pouch in advance. You can take it out of the container or more relaxed and throw it on the fire when you get to the site.

When packing with room in mind, plastic storage bags are often a handy measure. Packing additional storage bags for extra food after a meal is often a wise choice.

If they are not in their original box, do not forget to mark your pieces. Salt and sugar are easy to blend and taste entirely different!

If you are using reusable storage containers, Dry Erase Markers are excellent for marking. Go for the lasting magic marker if you are worried that it will come off. To know what order, you expect to cook each meal during the week, you can also want to number the meals. When you come to camp after a long day of sports, this also makes it much easier if you have some starving campers without the ability to find out what's for a meal.

Don't forget cooking utensils once you've scheduled your meals. Create a list of everything that you need for your cooking. The same utensils or cooking pots can be used for several of your things, but you want to make sure that you don't miss something. When cooking over an open fire, make sure to wear a pair of gloves. You may not have something set right above the fire, but it will still get sweltering if it is in the range of the flames, so remain vigilant! Also, prepare to wash your cooking utensils if you need to. A bowl for washing still comes in handy if you intend to use them for many meals. Using one, you emptied mostly during the preparation of that particular meal instead of packing a bowl just for drying. The same holds for storing leftover food; when you continue preparing your meals, you can end up with additional empty containers.

First but not least, always, every time, always carry your garbage bags to the camp with you. Carry as much as you think you'll need (for many uses, they come in handy, particularly if it rains!). We love the outdoors and want to preserve the perfect outdoors.

Going camping and finding that somebody has decided to throw their garbage on the field instead of pack out when they leave is frightening. Everyone should maintain a safe and healthy campground!!

Being imaginative is the secret to space conservation. When you become imaginative, several items can be used for separate work, minimizing the number of items you have to pack.

2.3. Dutch Oven Size

OVEN SIZE	OVEN CAPACITY	PERSONS SERVED
8-INCH	2 QUARTS	2-4
10-INCH	4 QUARTS	4-8
12-INCH	6 QUARTS	8-12
14-INCH	8 QUARTS	12-16
16-INCH	12 QUARTS	16-20

If you have bought your Dutch Oven, you will need to prepare it before using it for the first period. There are several multiple ways for your Oven to be prepared. One of the simplest ways to grease your Dutch Oven with vegetable shortening, particularly for first time Dutch Oven users, is to bake it in a traditional oven for one hour at 300 degrees. It is typically better for both the inside and outside the Oven to be greased to be thoroughly baked. Put a baking sheet lined with aluminum foil below the Dutch Oven to collect any drippings and cut back on cleaning during the seasoning phase.

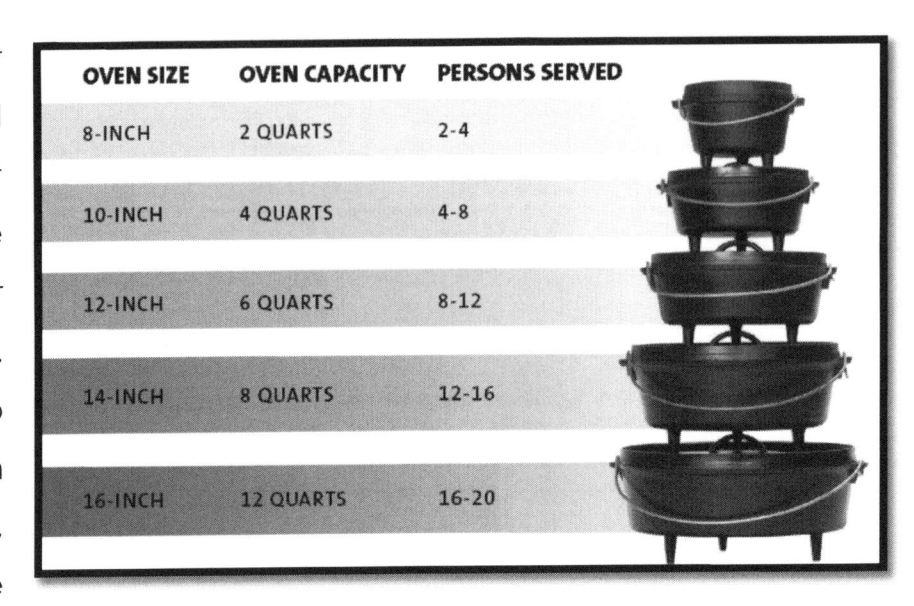

You will need a few tools before cooking in your Dutch Oven to make sure you don't get burnt in the cooking phase. You will need a stand to keep the Oven off the ground if your Oven has no foot on the rim. To check your food regularly to see if it is finished, a pair of gloves and a long-handled lid remover are essential.

You can cook until you have all of the required things and your Oven has been seasoned.

Over an open flame, named wood fire cooking, you can use the Dutch Oven, but managing the heat can be challenging. The most popular and simplest cooking method in a Dutch oven is to use briquettes for cooking to regulate the heat setting during the cooking phase. How much briquettes will be required will decide the size of the Oven. You would need to put briquettes in a complete circle on both the top and the Oven's bottom to warm the Oven to the correct temperature. Below is a map showing the number of briquettes required to achieve the correct temperature at the top of the Oven and the Oven base.

2.4. Packing Your Cool Box or Esky

One of camping's many joys is that it helps you get down to roots for a while and enjoy a comfortable lifestyle. However, the downside to this is that anytime you want cheese for your burger or an ice-cold brew, you can't just reach into the refrigerator.

Plus, to stop it from going off, you need to pay careful thought to how you can keep your food. The cool box used for drinks at your picnic on Sunday afternoon will not cut it for a camping trip of three to four days, as the walls are not adequately insulated. Invest in a decent cool package or esky and ice packs, both available from an outdoor or camping shop.

It would help keep your food cold and make it easy to find items, and keep them in good shape by giving a little thought to how you pack your cold meals while you go.

- Freeze some milk, juices, and water bottles you're going to be taking with you. For the first day or so, these will make excellent ice packs and freeze.

- Freeze the bacon, sausages, and beef packs before you go. It not only helps them last indefinitely until going off, but the frozen packets even serve like extra packs of ice.

- Put any snacks or meals you make in advance into sealed bags (see chapters 1 and 2), and then freeze them. For this, deliver containers perform correctly and can be neatly packed in your cool package. They can also do an equal thing for the trip to an ice pack. Do not try to remove the one for dinner that you intend to eat so that it defrosts in time!

- To stop them from being squashed, pack cheeses into shallow storage containers. Do the same for beef boxes. To avoid cross-contamination, keep items wrapped well.

- Several butchers can vacuum pack beef for a small fee, so inquire about this when ordering your meat. While the meat would also need to be packed in a cold box, it can last longer than unopened meat for an additional three to four days. If you have some healthy meat that won't last for another day, roast it and then cool it and enjoy it for lunch the next day.

- Use ice packs of high quality and make space for a sheet of them at the top of your cool box, as the cold air will sink in.

2.5. Packing Non-Perishable Foods

It often takes a little moral courage and preparation to pack all the things not placed

inside your cool box since space at the campsite is always at a premium. When you arrive, you can also save yourself a lot of time and resources if you have the following points.

- Save a storage container of little tomato ketchup pouches, soy sauce, sugar, salt, and other seasonings that always come with weekend takeout meals and shorter camping trips. It's safer to take standard bottles and jars for longer journeys since there is less packaging to dispose of.

- Write the contents using a washable marker on the top of your bins since you will be rummaging through boxes more often than not to find stuff, and the cover will be the easiest to locate. To conveniently find them in your food supply, stick white stickers on the tops of spice pots.

- Once you leave home, consider dissolving any ingredients into smaller packages, depending on how long you will be gone and how many individuals you will need to eat. One morning, if you think that you're going to make pancakes, measure the flour and baking powder, place it in an airtight jar or re-sealable lunch bag, and mark it to precisely know what it is for when you get to the campground. However, all you have to do is add your milk and eggs, and you're ready for cooking.

- While you could take a bottle of store-bought salad dressing, think about making some up when you go. It lasts well if you don't need it all on your ride, and you can still use it at household. A dressing is only a blend of olive oil and vinegar at its finest, one portion vinegar to two or three sections oil and some salt and pepper. If you like, add in a peeled garlic clove and a teaspoon of mustard.

2.6. Essential Food Items

Any of this book's recipes have a 'don't forget' trick to guarantee you have all the ingredients you need to taste as good as it does for the meal. It typically applies to storing kitchen cupboard ingredients that in a just last packing frenzy might be missed. You can't just pop out to the corner store while you're camping out in the woods. Nothing is worse than beginning to cook a meal and find that you've forgotten an essential element. I have suggested things here that I usually pack. I have no dedicated camping stuff, but instead, I take it from my kitchen cabinets because I realize it's new.

Condiments: Tomato sauce, mayonnaise, spaghetti, or sauce for pizza. Either carry the ones you have in your freezer or purchase smaller bottles or jars that take up less room if you shop specifically for your ride.

Butter: instead of the blocks covered in foil, I take some cashew cheese in a container as it stores more efficiently and is less likely to be found melting at the bottom of the cool package.

Capers and Olives: These two ingredients will change a recipe instantly. In salads, pasta, sauces, and dressings, I love them.

Cheese: Pack an assortment. I typically buy a pre-sliced bag to make it easy to cook sandwiches, and then a bag of grated cheese for pasta and pizza. And for the camp-fired warmed cheese, don't forget the decadent wheel of brie or camembert.

Chutney: Perfect for a fast baste or marinade, chutney elevates something a little more unique to a humble sandwich.

Cereals: As a basic guideline, I wouldn't say I like consuming delicious breakfast cereals, but I buy the range packs or mini cereals available at most supermarkets as a treat and convenience every few camping trips. The kids enjoy this treat not only, but I have an ulterior motive, less washing up! I carefully open the boxes and plastic inserts at the tip, then pour the milk straight in. The children enjoy the fun part of it, and a spoon is all that's left to wipe up.

Cold Meats: Carry a variety of sliced ham, salami, and chicken, and they can be used for pizzas and tortilla roll-ups, and sandwich fillings.

Herbs: Cooking and packing them before you leave home is the perfect way to transport and prepare fresh herbs for a camping trip. Shake out the residue and cover it in a wet paper towel. Scrub under the cool spray. Place in a small airtight container and store until you set off in the refrigerator, then store once required in your cool cabinet.

Milk: Many visitors take with them long-lasting milk. Before I go, I prefer storing organic milk to ensure it lasts longer. If you can, buy bottles with lids rather than a carton to stop leaks in your cooker box.

Oil: To save room, take one oil and use it for all-frying, marinades, bastes, and dressings.

Pesto: Suitable for fast sauces with spaghetti, to be used in marinades and stirred in soups. I'm satisfied with a decent quality store-bought container of pesto for camping, but make the own by all way before you go if users prefer.

Bread, Rolls, and Pita Pockets: Nice for morning toast, for lunch sandwiches, for mopping curries and stews, or for making calzone pizza or some of the kebabs. Marmalade, Vegemite, jelly, peanut butter, and sugar. Breakfast Spreads. Often, handy to have if you're preparing pancakes for breakfast.

2.7. Salad Ingredients

For me, protecting salad leaves from being squashed is an uphill task! To keep the greens fresh, bring complete lettuces, store them at the top of your cool box, or take pre-packaged packets, clean the leaves when you go, and store them in sealed bags with a sheet of wet paper towel at the back. Hold it in a cool package.

Salt and Pepper: I'm going to take a little bottle of sea salt (labeled at the top) and one of those grinders of disposable Pepper found in supermarkets' spice racks.

Spices: I still take the simple flavorings, like ground cumin, cilantro, paprika, or cayenne Pepper for sure. For stews, marinades, soups, and salad dressings, they easily incorporate extra spice.

Sugar: You won't need a full packet if you drink sugar in your tea or coffee, so decant it into a little glass. Label this precisely enough that you don't mistake it for salt!

2.8. Tea, Coffee and Hot Chocolate

We enjoy healthy coffee, which does not mean that you need to resort to instant coffee from a container because you're camping. Take either a plunger or an espresso maker with a stovetop, which you can put over the flames. For chilly mornings in winters and early evenings, hot chocolate is suitable.

Vinegar: For savory dishes, pack your preferred vinegar. My preference will be balsamic or wine vinegar.

Water: Some campgrounds have no access to water possible, especially the more distant bush ones. Before you go, search. They're also by a river where you can shower and get water to wash up, but you're going to have to drink and boil all of your water. Before you go, buy a pair of 25-liter water tanks and fill them at home. When you are at the campground, keep water in the shade to stay cool for drinking.

2.9. Camping Cooking Utensils

Most campers carry boxes of utensils in the shed for camp. While I only have a range of melamine crockery, for this reason, I find it easier to determine what I'm making preparations for, then take from my storage boxes the appropriate utensils.

32

You'll also need cutlery, crockery, cups, and glasses for all, as well as the items mentioned below. I used those plates that had different containers when my kids were little. I find them better because they seem to have a lip across the side, meaning less food falls out if you eat sitting in a chair rather than at a table.

1. Bowls

For preparing and serving salads, one large thin plastic bowl, a medium-sized bowl, and a few small bowls for producing salad dressings and marinade look for sustainable and

environment washing up liquid in outdoor shops and keep it with your camping supplies. I even take a big plastic bowl or tub for washing up.

2. Chopping Boards

Take one or two chopping boards made of plastic.

3. Scissors

If you don't use sliced bread, take one little and one moderate sharp knife and a bread knife.

4. Lighter

A gas stove burner is more powerful and safer than matches, but it is useful to have waterproof matches.

5. Pans

Bring up a frying pan, a big saucepan, and a medium saucepan.

6. Peeler

Peeling is better than washing certain vegetables and fruits since water can also be scarce.

7. Sieve

At a camping shop, I find a collapsible sieve. It packs flat, but on every ride, it comes now.

8. Skewers

Wooden or metal keeps them from burning during cooking; note to soak wooden skewers beforehand.

9. Spade

Not exclusively cooking equipment, but required as you'll need to shift the coals around while cooking with coals.

10. Spoons

For serving and stirring, take a pair of large spoons, metal or plastic.

11. Tea Towels

Or you might choose an ovenproof mitt to cook around the fire for washing up and holding hot pans.

12. Opener

And don't worry about the bottle opener as well!

13. Tongs

Not only handy for barbecue but also handy for salad tossing.

14. Torch

But not purely cooking machinery; when cooking at night, keep your head torch at hand.

Chapter 3: Camping Main Dishes

In this chapter, we will provide you with Main Dishes that you can cook while camping.

3.1. Parmigiana Chicken

(Serving 6, Cook Time: 2–6 hours, Difficulty: Hard)

Ingredients:

- 1 egg
- 1 tsp. salt
- ¼ tsp. pepper
- 6 bone-in, skinless chicken breast halves
- 1 cup Italian bread crumbs
- 2–4 Tbsp. butter
- 14-oz. jar of your favorite pizza sauce
- 6 slices mozzarella cheese grated Parmesan cheese

Instructions:

1. Beat the egg, salt, and pepper together in a low-sided dish, wide enough to dip half

the chicken breast into it.

2. In another low-sided dish, incorporate bread crumbs, also wide enough to accommodate half a chicken breast.

3. Dip half of each breast into the egg mixture. Uh, drain.

4. Dip each half of the breast into bread crumbs to cover the two sides

5. Meanwhile, melt the pan with sugar. Lightly brown each breast in the butter in the skillet on both sides. You might place a couple at once in the pan; make sure you don't crowd the skillet because they're not going to brown.

6. Arrange the slow cooker with the browned chicken.

7. Pizza sauce with a spoon over chicken.

8. Stove cover. Cook on a meat thermometer stuck in the middle of the breast for 4-6 hours or until chicken registers 165° but did not hit any bone.

9. Layer and line with mozzarella cheese and scatter with Parmesan cheese. Cook uncovered, only before you melt the cheese.

3.2. Basil Chicken

(Serving 4-6, Cook Time: 4½ hours, Difficulty: Hard)

Ingredients:

- 2 pounds boneless, skinless chicken thighs
- 14½-oz. can diced tomatoes with juice
- 14½-oz can garbanzo beans, drained and rinsed
- 2 Tbsp. capers with their brine
- 2 garlic cloves, sliced thinly
- ⅛ tsp. freshly ground black pepper
- 1 tsp. dried basil
- 8 oz. crumbled feta cheese

- ¼ cup tightly packed basil leaves, chopped

Instructions:

1. Put the chicken in a slow cooking oven. On top, pour onions, garbanzos, and capers.

2. Sprinkle with slices of garlic, dried basil, and pepper.

3. Cover and simmer for under 4 hours.

4. Sprinkle feta over it. For 15-30 more minutes, or until the chicken is cooked, cook on medium.

5. Sprinkle and serve with fresh basil. Useful for treating the sauce with spaghetti or crusty rolls.

3.3. French Chicken

(Serving 4-6, Cook Time: 4½–5½ Hours, Difficulty: Hard)

- 1 lb. baby carrots
- 2 medium onions, sliced
- 2 ribs celery, diced
- 4 garlic cloves, peeled
- 3 lbs. bone-in chicken thighs, skin removed
- *½ cup white cooking wine or chicken stock
- 1½ tsp. salt
- ½ tsp. black pepper
- 1 tsp. dried basil
- ½ tsp. dried marjoram
- 2 Tbsp. chopped fresh parsley

Instructions:

1. Place carrots, onions, celery, and garlic in the bottom of the slow cooker.

2. Lay chicken thighs on top. Pour wine or broth over chicken.

3. Sprinkle with salt, pepper, basil, and marjoram.

4. Cover. Cook on Low 4½–5½ hours, until chicken registers 165° on a meat thermometer and carrots are tender.

5. Sprinkle with fresh parsley before serving. Why I like this recipe — It is tempting to have a little French daydream when you make this chicken. It's straightforward, but the flavor is lovely—isn't that how the French cook?

3.4. Simple Chicken Thighs

(Serving 4-6, Cook Time: 4–6 Hours, Difficulty: Hard)

Ingredients:

- 2 lbs. bone-in chicken thighs, skin removed
- 2 Tbsp. olive oil
- 3 Tbsp. red wine vinegar
- ¼ cup honey
- ¼ cup soy sauce 1 garlic clove, minced
- ½ tsp. freshly ground pepper
- ¼ cup chopped fresh parsley

Instructions:

1. Place a single layer of chicken in a shallow glass pan.

2. Combine the oil, sugar, butter, soya sauce, garlic, pepper, and parsley in a shallow dish.

3. Pour chicken over it. Marinate for at least 3 hours and up to 12 in the fridge.

4. In a slow cooker, put the chicken with the marinade. Heat and cook for 4-6 hours on the low side.

5. Either raise and eat the chicken thighs from the resulting sauce, or thicken it with a 1-Tbsp. mixture, cornstarch and 3 Tbsp. The water combined, then whisked through the hot sauce.

6. Serve the thickened sauce as a side gravy.

3.5. Favorite Honey Chicken

(Serving 6, Cook Time: 4 Hours, Difficulty: Hard)

Ingredients:

- 6 boneless, skinless chicken thighs half a small onion, sliced in rings
- 4 Tbsp. butter
- ½ cup honey
- ¼ cup prepared mustard
- ½ tsp. salt
- 1 tsp. curry powder

Instructions:

1. Clean the chicken and pat it dry. Just put it in a slow cooker. Separate the onions and divide them among the chicken parts into separate rings.

2. In the oven, heat the butter. Mix and spill over the chicken with the remaining ingredients.

3. Heat and cook for 4 hours on low or before chicken on a meat thermometer registers 165°. Place the chicken and the sauce on a rimmed baking sheet and run under the broiler to get some brown spots on the chicken and bubbly sauce if you have time and inclination.

3.6. Chicken Cacciatore

(Serves 6, Cook Time 5-6 Hour, Difficulty: Normal)

Ingredients:

- 3 lbs. bone-in chicken pieces, skin removed
- 2 green bell peppers, thinly sliced
- 2 medium onions, thinly sliced
- 2 garlic cloves, thinly sliced
- ½ lb. fresh mushrooms, sliced
- ½ tsp. dried rosemary
- 1 tsp. dried oregano
- ½ tsp. dried basil
- 1 tsp. salt
- ¼ tsp. pepper, freshly ground
- 1 Tbsp. balsamic vinegar
- 1 cup tomato sauce
- 3 cups chopped tomatoes
- 3 oz. tomato paste
- 2-oz. can sliced black olives, drained
- ¾ cup chopped fresh basil, optional hot cooked spaghetti

Instructions:

1. Lay the pieces of chicken on a slow cooker. Add the tomatoes, onions, mushrooms, and garlic.

2. Mix the rosemary, oregano, dried basil, salt, pepper, vinegar, tomato sauce, tomato paste, and tomato paste in a cup.

3. Pour the tomato mixture over the chicken and vegetables

4. Cover and cook for 5-6 hours on medium until the chicken is soft and done.

5. Serve in soup bowls, sprinkled with olives and optional basil, with chicken bits and sauce across spaghetti.

3.7. Asian Chicken Breast

(Serves 4, Cook Time 20-30 Minutes, Difficulty: Normal)

Ingredients:

- 1 Tbsp. sesame oil
- 1 Tbsp. rice vinegar or white wine vinegar
- 3 Tbsp. soy sauce
- 3 Tbsp. honey fresh ground pepper, to taste
- 2" piece ginger root, chopped, peeled or not
- 1 lb. boneless skinless chicken breasts
- 2 spring onions, chopped
- 3 Tbsp. sesame seeds, toasted

Instructions:

1. Mix the veggie broth, vinegar, soy sauce, honey, and pepper until soft.

2. In a slow cooker, put the chicken and ginger together. Pour sauce on top and spread it thinly to scatter.

3. Cover until chicken is just done, then cook on low for 4 hours.

4. To eat a salad, cut the chicken and sauce. Sprinkle with sesame seeds and spring onions. It is beautifully served with hot rice.

3.8. Orange Ginger Wings

(Serves 4, Cook Time 30 Minutes, Difficulty: Normal)

Ingredients:

- 2 pounds chicken wings
- 1 tablespoon ginger,
- grated ½ cup soy sauce
- ¼ cup honey
- ¼ cup orange juice
- ½ teaspoon red pepper
- ½ teaspoon black pepper

Instructions:

1. Combine the ginger, 1/4 cup of the soy, orange juice, black pepper, and red pepper.

2. Marinate the chicken wings in orange-ginger sauce for an hour.

3. Fire the grill and cook the chicken wings, turning twice and turning twice, for 20 minutes.

4. Pair the sugar with the remaining soy sauce, then drizzle over the wings.

5. Serve with celery and carrot sticks or your side pick.

3.9. Herbed Chicken

(Serves 4-6, Cook Time 2 Hours, Difficulty: Normal)

Ingredients:

- 5-lb. roasting chicken
- 1 onion, quartered
- 2 garlic cloves:
- 1 sliced, 1 whole
- 1 Tbsp. fresh parsley, or 1 tsp. dried

- 1 Tbsp. fresh sage, or 1 tsp. dried
- 1 Tbsp. fresh rosemary, or 1 tsp. dried
- 1 Tbsp. fresh thyme, or 1 tsp. dried
- 1 Tbsp. butter, softened paprika to taste salt to taste pepper to taste

Instructions:

1. Clean the chicken and wash it. Dry Pat.

2. In the bird's cavity, put the quartered onion and chopped garlic. Stuff yourself with parsley, sage, rosemary, and thyme.

3. Rub the entire garlic clove on the outside of the chicken and then throw it into the cavity.

4. With softened butter, rub the exterior of the chicken. I am using paprika, salt, and pepper to sprinkle.

5. Put the chicken in a slow cooker with grease.

6. Uh. Cover. Cook for 4-6 hours or until the meat is tender, the drumsticks pass freely, and the juices are pure.

7. Lift the chicken onto a plate from the oven. To stay warm, cover with foil. Before you break it up, let it rest for 15 minutes.

8. To make gravy, thicken the chicken stock. Or make rice with the broth

3.10. Herby Chicken with Pesto

(Serves 6-8, Cook Time 1 Hour, Difficulty: Normal)

Ingredients:

Pesto Ingredients:

- 2 cups fresh basil, or 2 Tbsp. dried basil
- ½ cup olive oil
- 2 Tbsp. pine nuts

- 2 cloves garlic, crushed
- 1 tsp. salt
- ½ cup Parmesan cheese, freshly grated
- 2 Tbsp. Romano cheese, grated
- 3 Tbsp. butter, softened

Chicken Ingredients:

- 6 medium onions, coarsely chopped
- 2 Tbsp. olive oil
- 2 28-oz. cans plum tomatoes, undrained
- 1 Tbsp. fresh thyme, or 1 tsp. dried thyme
- 1 Tbsp. fresh basil, or 1 tsp. dried basil
- 1 Tbsp. fresh tarragon, or 1 tsp. dried tarragon
- 1 Tbsp. fresh rosemary, or 1 tsp. fresh rosemary
- 4 cloves fresh garlic, minced
- *2 cups chicken broth
- 4 cups dry white wine
- 2–3 lbs. chicken thighs, bone in, skin removed
- 1½–2 lbs. small new potatoes, unpeeled
- 2 loaves French bread, sliced and warmed

Instructions:

1. Make the pesto first. Blend all of its ingredients, except the cheeses and softened butter, in a blender or food processor. Pour the mixture into a bowl and then stir in the cheeses and butter.

2. Put the onions, olive oil, tomatoes with their juice, all the herbs, the garlic, chicken broth, wine, and half the pesto into your slow cooker. Mix everything well.

3. Nestle the chicken thighs into the tomato-y broth, submerging them as much as you can.

4. Add the potatoes, pushing them down into the broth, too. 5. Cover. Cook on Low 4–6 hours, or until the potatoes are soft when you jag

they with a fork, and the chicken is tender.

6. Serve in deep soup plates with plenty of hot French bread to mop up the juices. Serve the remaining pesto at the table.

3.11. Creamy Chicken in Gravy

(Serves 6, Cook Time 1-2 Hours, Difficulty: Normal)

Ingredients:

- 6 large bone-in chicken thighs, skin removed
- *10¾-oz. can cream of broccoli, or broccoli cheese, soup
- *10¾-oz. can cream of chicken soup
- ½ cup white wine
- ½ tsp. dried thyme
- ¼ tsp. dried sage pinch dried rosemary pinch black pepper
- ¼ lb. fresh mushrooms, sliced, or 4-oz. can sliced mushrooms, undrained

Instructions:

1. Place chicken thighs in the slow cooker.

2. In a bowl, mix soups, wine, herbs, and mushroom slices. Pour over chicken.

3. Cover. Cook on Low 4–5 hours, or until chicken is tender but not dry.

4. Serve over rice or noodles.

3.12. Chicken with Raisins and Rice

(Serves 8, Cook Time 30 Minutes, Difficulty: Normal)

Ingredients:

- 3 cups unsalted, low-fat chicken broth
- 1½ cups uncooked, long-grain white rice
- ¾ cup raisins
- ½ cup chopped onion 2–3 lbs. chicken thighs, bone in, skin removed
- ½ cup all-purpose flour
- 1 Tbsp. curry powder
- ½ tsp. salt
- ½ cup chopped peanuts
- ½ cup chopped peanuts

Instructions:

1. Combine chicken broth, rice, raisins, and onions in your greased slow cooker.

2. Combine flour, curry, and salt in a sturdy plastic bag without any holes or tears. Add chicken thighs, one at a time, to the bag and shake until well coated. Lay each piece in the rice mixture, pushing it down until it's as submerged as possible.

3. Cover. Cook on Low 4–5 hours, or High 2–3 hours.

4. Lift the chicken onto a platter. Cover with foil to keep warm. Stir the peanuts into the rice. Put the chicken back into the cooker. Cover and cook ½ hour longer.

3.13. Chicken Breasts Stuffed with Pesto

(Serves 6, Cook Time 30 Minutes, Difficulty: Normal)

Ingredients:

- 6 boneless, skinless chicken breasts, not more than

- 4 lbs. total
- ½ cup chopped fresh basil
- 6 garlic cloves
- ⅓ cup extra-virgin olive oil
- ½ cup grated Parmesan cheese
- ¾ cup fresh bread crumbs hot water, optional
- 2 Tbsp. pine nuts watercress, optional

Instructions:

1. Flatten each chicken breast by pounding between two wax paper sheets until they're each ½" thick. Lay each one on a square, buttered piece of tin foil, shiny side up.

2. In a food processor, mix basil, garlic, and olive oil. Pulse several times to chop and blend the ingredients.

3. Add cheese and bread crumbs. Process until the mixture forms a paste. Add a little bit of hot water if you need it to make the paste spreadable. Add the pine nuts and pulse to chop.

4. Divide the basil mixture among the 8-breasts. Place a spoonful on the center of each breast. Roll up each stuffed breast jelly-roll style. Wrap the square of foil tightly around each one to hold the goodies inside.

5. Stack the foil packages of chicken evenly in the cooker. Cook 4–6 hours on Low. After 4 hours, lift a pack out of the cooker and open it carefully. Open the package so that the steam is directed away from yourself. Stick the quick-read meat thermometer into the center of the breast (be sure you're against meat and not the filling). If the thermometer registers 165°, the chicken is finished. If it's less than that, wrap it up, put it back in the cooker, and continue cooking for another 30 minutes. Repeat the check.

6. When the chicken is done cooking, remove each breast from the foil. Slice it into 1"-thick slices, fanning them over a dinner plate. Spoon some cooking juices over the top.

7. If you want, sprinkle some fresh watercress leaves over the top before serving.

3.14. Curried Chicken and Fruit

(Serves 5, Cook Time 30 Minutes, Difficulty: Normal)

Ingredients:

- 2½–3½ lbs. chicken thighs, bone in, skin removed
- ½ tsp. salt
- ¼ tsp. pepper
- 1–2 Tbsp. curry powder, depending on how much you like curry
- 1 garlic clove, crushed or minced
- 1 Tbsp. butter, melted
- *½ cup chicken broth, or 1 chicken bouillon cube dissolved in ½ cup water
- 2 Tbsp. finely chopped onion 29-oz. can sliced peaches
- ½ cup pitted prunes
- 3 Tbsp. cornstarch
- 3 Tbsp. cold water
- Cooked rice, for serving peanuts, shredded coconut, and fresh pineapple chunks, optional, for serving

Instructions:

1. Place chicken in slow cooker.

2. Combine salt, pepper, curry powder, garlic, butter, broth, and onions in bowl.

3. Drain peaches, reserving syrup. Add ½ cup syrup to curry mixture. Pour over chicken.

4. Cover. Cook on Low 4–5 hours. Remove chicken from slow cooker. Tent with foil to keep warm.

5. Turn cooker on High. Stir prunes into sauce in cooker.

6. In a small bowl, dissolve cornstarch in cold water. Stir into hot broth in slow cooker.

7. Cover. Cook on High 10 minutes, stirring once or twice, or until thickened. Add peaches. Add cooked chicken. (You can debone the chicken if you want.)

8. Serve over cooked rice. Offer peanuts, shredded coconut, and fresh pineapple chunks as condiments.

3.15. Wild Rice with Chicken

(Serves 8-10, Cook Time 1 Hour, Difficulty: Normal)

Ingredients:

- 2 cups wild rice, uncooked
- ½ cup chopped onions
- ½ cup chopped celery
- 2 cups uncooked skinless chicken thighs, cut in 1-inch pieces
- *6 cups chicken stock
- ¼–½ tsp. salt, depending how salty your stock is
- ¼ tsp. pepper
- ¼ tsp. garlic powder
- ½ tsp. dried sage
- 8–12-oz. canned mushrooms, drained, or ½ lb. fresh mushrooms, sliced
- ½ cup slivered almonds
- 2 Tbsp. fresh parsley

Instructions:

1. Wash and drain the rice.

2. Combine all ingredients, except mushrooms, almonds, and parsley, in the greased slow cooker. Mix well.

3. Cover. Cook on Low 4–8 hours, or until rice is tender. Don't lift the lid to check on things until the rice has cooked 4-hours.

4. Ten minutes before the end of the cooking time, stir in the mushrooms. Cover and continue cooking.

5. Just before serving, stir in slivered almonds. Garnish with fresh parsley.

3.16. Sunny Chicken

(Serves 4-5, Cook Time 35-40 Minutes, Difficulty: Normal)

Ingredients:

- 1 large onion, sliced into thin rings, divided
- 3 sweet, juicy oranges, each cut into thin slices, divided
- 3 lemons, thinly sliced, divided
- 3 limes, thinly sliced, divided
- 9 fresh rosemary sprigs, divided
- 2 Tbsp. minced garlic, divided
- 5-lb. chicken
- salt and pepper to taste

Instructions:

1. Layer ⅓ of the onion slices, 1-sliced orange, 1-sliced lemon, and 1-sliced lime into your slow cooker. Top with 3-rosemary sprigs and ⅓ of the minced garlic.

2. Stuff with half the remaining onion slices, 1-sliced orange, 1-sliced lemon, and 1-sliced lime, half the remaining garlic, and 3-rosemary sprigs. Place the stuffed chicken—upside down—in your slow cooker. (That helps to keep the breast meat from drying out.)

3. Sprinkle with plenty of salt and pepper. Spread the rest of the onion, orange, lemon, and lime slices, and the remaining garlic and rosemary sprig around the chicken and on top of it.

4. Cover. Cook on Low 4–6 hours, or until meat is tender but not dry.

5. Remove chicken from cooker and place right side up on the rimmed baking sheet. Place under broiler until top is nicely browned, only a minute or so, watching closely.

6. Cover chicken with foil for 15 minutes. Then carve, put the pieces on a platter, and spoon the citrus and onion slices over the top before serving.

3.17. Cranberry Chicken

(Serves 6, Cook Time 40 Minutes, Difficulty: Normal)

Ingredients:

- 1 cup chopped onion
- 2 tsp. vegetable oil
- 6 boneless, skinless chicken breast halves
- ⅓ cup tomato sauce
- 1 Tbsp. cider vinegar
- 1 Tbsp. brown sugar
- 2 Tbsp. orange marmalade
- ½ cup dried cranberries
- ½ tsp. chili powder
- ½ tsp. ground allspice
- 1 tsp. salt
- ¼ tsp. freshly ground pepper

Instructions:

1. Place onion, oil, and a few chicken breasts halves in a large skillet. Brown the halves about 3 minutes on each side. Be careful not to crowd the skillet with the chicken, or it will steam, not brown.

2. Remove the onions if they are browned and place in the slow cooker. Brown the chicken in batches until all the halves are browned on both sides.

3. Mix remaining ingredients in a small bowl until smooth.

4. Pour sauce over chicken breasts.

5. Cover and cook on Low for about 4 hours, until chicken registers 165° on a meat thermometer stuck into the breasts' centers.

6. Serve over brown rice to catch and enjoy the lovely sauce.

3.18. Amish Filling

(Serves 8-12, Cook Time 3-4 Hours, Difficulty: Normal)

Ingredients:

- 1½ sticks (12 Tbsp.) butter
- 1½ sticks (12 Tbsp.) butter
- 1 medium onion, diced
- 2 cups diced celery
- 1½ tsp. salt
- ½ tsp. pepper
- 4 eggs, beaten
- *3–4 cups chicken broth, divided
- 18–20 slices bread (about 12–14 cups), cubed or torn
- 4 cups diced, cooked chicken, divided

Instructions:

1. Melt the butter in a large stockpot (you'll soon see why you need the big pot). Sauté the onion and celery, stirring often, until the vegetables are just softened. Stir in the salt and pepper.

2. In a medium-sized bowl, mix the eggs and 2 cups chicken broth together.

3. Put the bread pieces into a large bowl. Pour the eggs-and-broth mixture, and the butter with the sautéed onions and celery, over the bread cubes. Toss everything together until all of the bread is moistened.

4. Spoon the bread cubes into the large stockpot (that you used in Step 1) and fry over medium heat until lightly browned. Stir often so the bread cubes brown throughout and so none burn.

5. When the bread is nicely browned, spoon about ⅓ of it into your large, greased slow cooker.

6. Top it with half the chicken.

7. Put half the remaining bread into the slow cooker. Top with the rest of the chicken. Add the rest of the bread on top.

8. Pour 1 cup chicken broth across the top layer of bread. You can add more broth while the Filling cooks if you want it to stay really moist.

9. Cover. Cook on Low 3–4 hours. The longer the Filling cooks, the drier it will be. Or if you don't have time to let it cook longer but like it somewhat dry, take the lid off for the last 45 minutes of cooking.

3.19. "Stir-Fry" Chicken and Broccoli

(Serves 4, Cook Time 1 Hour, Difficulty: Normal)

Ingredients:

- 4 good-sized boneless, skinless chicken thighs
- 1–2 Tbsp. oil
- ½ cup picante sauce
- 2 Tbsp. soy sauce
- ½ tsp. sugar
- ½ Tbsp. quick-cooking tapioca
- 1 medium onion, chopped

- 2 garlic cloves, minced
- ½ tsp. ground ginger
- 2 cups broccoli florets
- 1 medium red bell pepper, cut into pieces

Instructions:

1. Cut chicken into 1" cubes and brown lightly in oil in a skillet. Place in the slow cooker.

2. Stir in the remaining ingredients.

3. Cover. Cook on High 1–1½ hours or Low 2–3 hours. 4. Serve over cooked white rice.

3.20. Cornish Game Hens with Bacon and New Potatoes

(Serves 4, Cook Time 2 Hours, Difficulty: Easy)

Ingredients:

- ½ tsp. salt
- 1 tsp. dried thyme
- 1 tsp. dried rosemary
- 2 garlic cloves, peeled
- 2 garlic cloves, peeled
- 2 carrots, scrubbed and cut in chunks
- 1½ cups small new potatoes, scrubbed and dried
- 4 slices bacon

Instructions:

1. Rub hens inside and out with salt, thyme, and rosemary. Place a garlic clove in each cavity.

2. Spread carrots and potatoes in the slow cooker. Lay the hens on top.

3. Lay the bacon slices in a cross on each hen, tucking the ends under.

4. Cover and cook on Low for 4–6 hours, or until legs move quickly when pulled on or twisted.

5. Before serving, brown and crisp the bacon by setting hens on a baking sheet and broiling for a minute or two, OR don't bother with the broiling and discard the bacon.

3.21. Mexican Supper-in-a-Crock

(Serves 8, Cook Time 1-2 Hour, Difficulty: Normal)

Ingredients:

- 1 cup uncooked brown rice
- *1½ cups chicken stock, and possibly
- ¼ cup more
- 1 lb. boneless, skinless chicken breast, cubed
- ¼ cup chopped onion
- 15-oz. can black beans, rinsed and drained
- 1 cup corn, canned, frozen, or fresh
- 4 garlic cloves, sliced thinly
- 1 cup diced red bell pepper
- 1 cup diced green bell pepper
- 14½-oz. can diced tomatoes, undrained
- 2 tsp. ground cumin
- 1 Tbsp. chili powder
- ½ tsp. salt, or less, depending on how salty your stock is
- ¼ tsp. pepper
- 1½ cups shredded Monterey Jack or pepper Jack cheese
- ½ cup chopped cilantro, for garnish

Instructions:

1. Pour together the rice and 1 1/2 cups of stock into a lightly greased crock.

2. Next, add the chicken cubes, followed by the onion, black beans, corn, red pepper, garlic, and green pepper.

3. Stir the onions, cumin, chili powder, salt, and pepper together in a separate dish. Over the contents of the crock, spill equally.

4. Cover and simmer for 3 hours on the high side.

5. To see if the rice is finished, politely poke a knife down to the floor. Add the cheese on top and cook an extra 15 minutes until the cheese is nicely cooked, whether it is. Add 1/4 cup of hot water or hot stock and cook an extra 30 minutes on high if the rice is already a little crunchy and there is no liquid left. Then add the cheese and leave for 15 minutes to melt.

6. Just before eating, sprinkle with chopped cilantro.

3.22. Arroz con Pollo

(Serves 6-8, Cook Time 2 Hours, Difficulty: Normal)

Ingredients:

- 1 Tbsp. vegetable oil
- 4 strips bacon, chopped
- 2 cups uncooked, diced boneless, skinless chicken breast
- 1 onion, chopped 1 green bell pepper, chopped
- 2 cups long-grain white rice, uncooked
- 3⅓ cups chicken broth
- 3 cloves garlic, minced
- ½ cup chopped fresh cilantro
- ¼ tsp. pepper

- 1 tsp. dried oregano
- 1 tsp. chili powder
- ½ tsp. turmeric
- ½ cup tomato sauce
- ½ cup sliced green olives
- 1 cup frozen peas, thawed

Instructions:

1. Add Oil to skillet. Add bacon, chicken, onion, pepper, and rice. Fry for several minutes to allow the bacon to crisp up and chicken to get browned spots. Stir well to coat the rice. Allow to brown for a few more minutes without stirring.

2. Scrape sauté into the slow cooker, being sure to get all drippings and browned bits.

3. Add chicken broth, garlic, cilantro, pepper, oregano, chili powder, turmeric, and tomato sauce. Stir.

4. Cover and cook on High for 1½–2½ hours, until rice is tender and liquid is absorbed.

5. Use a fork to gently stir in olives and peas, fluffing up rice as you go. Allow resting, covered, for a few minutes before serving.

3.23. Tex-Mex Chicken Roll-ups

(Serves 6, Cook Time 2 Hours, Difficulty: Normal)

Ingredients:

- 6 boneless, skinless chicken breast halves, about 1½ lbs.
- 6 oz. Monterey Jack cheese, cut into 2"-long, ½"-thick sticks
- 2 4-oz. cans chopped green chilies, drained
- ¾ cup flour
- ½ cup (1 stick) butter, melted
- ½ cup dry bread crumbs

- ¼ cup grated Parmesan cheese
- 1 Tbsp. chili powder pinch cayenne, optional
- ½ tsp. salt
- ½ tsp. ground cumin

Instruction:

1. Cover each chicken breast with plastic wrap, and on a cutting board, flatten each with a mallet to ⅛" thickness.

2. Place a cheese stick in the middle of each and top with a mound of chilies. Roll up and tuck in ends. Secure with a toothpick. Set aside each breast half on a platter.

3. Place flour in a shallow dish and melted butter in another.

4. In yet another shallow dish, mix bread crumbs, Parmesan cheese, chili powder, optional cayenne, salt, and cumin.

5. Now take the chicken roll-ups and dip each one in flour, then melted butter, then the crumb mixture.

6. Place seam-side down in a single layer in the greased slow cooker.

7. Cook on Low for 4–4½ hours, until chicken registers 165° on a meat thermometer.

8. Gently transfer chicken rolls to a rimmed baking sheet. Place them under a broiler until crumbs are crispy and slightly browned. Observe!

9. Be sure to remove toothpicks before serving, or else give your diners a heads-up.

3.24. Italian Chicken Fajita Wraps
(Serves 4-6, Cook Time 2 Hours, Difficulty: Normal)

- 1 lb. boneless, skinless chicken breasts
- 2 garlic cloves, sliced thinly
- 2 Tbsp. dried oregano
- 1 Tbsp. dried parsley

- 1 tsp. dried basil
- ½ tsp. dried thyme
- ¼ tsp. celery seed
- 1 Tbsp. sugar
- ½ tsp. salt
- 1 tsp. freshly ground pepper
- 8-oz. bottle Italian salad dressing
- 1 cup salsa
- 1 green bell pepper, sliced in ribs
- 1 red bell pepper, sliced in ribs
- 1 medium onion, sliced in rings
- 10 10"-flour tortillas

Toppings, Choose All or Some:

- freshly grated Parmesan cheese
- fresh mozzarella slices
- hot sauce, or pickled Italian hot peppers
- chopped olives
- lemon wedges
- shredded lettuce chopped
- tomatoes chopped
- fresh basil

Instructions:

1. Split into small pieces of chicken. Could you place it in a big mixing bowl?

2. Combine the garlic, spices, salt, cinnamon, pepper, salad dressing, and salsa. Mix thoroughly. Cover and marinate in the fridge for 4–8 hours or overnight.

3. Pour the marinade and chicken into a slow cooker. Cook for 2-4 hours on medium, until the center and tender chicken, is white.

4. Spoon the chicken and its sauce into a serving dish or rimmed baking sheet that is oven-proof. Attach some vegetables. Slide it for a few minutes under the broiler until the chicken and vegetables have browned patches.

5. Serve with toppings and tortillas and plenty of napkins.

3.25. Turkey with Mushroom Sauce
(Serves 12, Cook Time 2 Hours, Difficulty: Normal)

Ingredients:

- 2 lbs. boneless skinless turkey thighs, cut in 2" chunks
- 1 medium onion, chopped
- 3 cups sliced mushrooms
- 3 Tbsp. butter
- 2 Tbsp. soy sauce
- *½ cup beef stock
- 1 tsp. poultry seasoning
- ¼ cup all-purpose flour
- ½ cup water
- ¼ cup chopped fresh parsley

Instructions:

1. Place turkey, onions, mushrooms, butter, soy sauce, stock, and poultry seasoning in the slow cooker.

2. Cover and cook on Low for 4 hours.

3. Whisk together flour and water until smooth. Pour into hot mixture in the slow cooker, stirring continuously until blended. A small whisk will work for this.

4. Cover and cook an additional 30 minutes on Low, until sauce is thickened and hot. Check flavor and add a bit more poultry seasoning or salt if needed.

5. Garnish with parsley. Serve over broad egg noodles or next to a rice pilaf.

3.26. King Turkey

(Serves 10-12, Cook Time1-2 Hour, Difficulty: Normal)

Ingredients:

- 5-to 6-lb. turkey breast, bone in and skin on
- 1 medium onion, chopped
- 1 rib celery, chopped
- half stick (¼ cup) melted butter
- a good shower of salt to taste
- a sprinkling of lemon pepper to taste
- *1 cup chicken broth 1 cup white wine

Instructions:

1. Wash the breast of the turkey. Dry Pat. Place the celery and onion in the cavity. Place the slow cooker in greased Oil.

2. Over turkey, pour melted butter. With salt and lemon pepper, season.

3. Pour the water over the turkey and the wine.

4. Uh. Cover. Cook for 5-7 hours or until 165° is reported by the meat thermometer. (Make sure the thermometer does not touch the bone.)

5. Let it stand before carving for 15 minutes.

3.27. Turkey Barbecue Makes

(Serves 10, Cook Time 1 Hour, Difficulty: Normal)

Ingredients:

- Ideal slow-cooker size: 6-quart
- 4-or 5-lb. turkey breast with the bone in olive oil
- 1–2 Tbsp. water

Barbecue Sauce:

- 3 Tbsp. butter
- 1 chopped onion
- 1 cup chicken broth
- ½–1 cup ketchup
- 1 tsp. salt dash pepper
- 2 Tbsp. apple cider vinegar
- 4–6 Tbsp. brown sugar
- 1 Tbsp. prepared mustard
- 1–2 Tbsp. Worcestershire sauce
- a few dashes of hot sauce

Instruction:

1. Rub the breast inside and out with olive oil.

2. Put the breast into your slow cooker.

3. Add the water.

4. Cover. Cook on Low 5–6 hours, or until the meat registers 165° in the center of the breast (but not touching the bone) on a quick-read thermometer.

5. Lift breast out of the cooker and let it cool. Then debone it. Cube the meat or shred it with two forks.

6. Use 1 cup of the broth in the Barbecue Sauce. Freeze the rest of the broth and use it to make soup or rice. Mix all ingredients for the Barbecue Sauce.

7. Put the meat back into the cooker.

8. Pour the sauce over the cut-up turkey and mix everything together well.

9. Cover. Heat on Low 2–3 hours, or until it's heated through. Then serve it on sandwich rolls that are sturdy enough to handle the sauce.

3.28. Creamy Turkey with Vegetables Dinner

(Serves 4-6, Cook Time 1-2 Hour, Difficulty: Normal)

Instructions:

- 1 onion, diced
- 6 small red potatoes, quartered
- 2 cups sliced carrots
- 2 lbs. boneless, skinless turkey thighs, cut into 4–6 pieces
- ¼ cup flour
- 2 Tbsp. (1 envelope) dry onion soup mix
- ½ tsp. dried sage
- ½ tsp. dried thyme
- 10¾-oz. can cream of mushroom soup
- ** ⅔ cup chicken broth, or water

Instruction:

1. Place the vegetables in a slow cooker at the bottom.

2. Place the thighs of turkey over the vegetables.

3. Mix the remaining ingredients. Pour the turkey on.

4. Cover and simmer for less than 4-5 hours.

3.29. Barbecued Turkey Cutlets (with a great variation)

(Serves 6-8, Cook Time 1 Hour, Difficulty: Normal)

Ingredients:

- (1½–2 lbs.) turkey cutlets
- ¼ cup molasses
- ¼ cup apple cider vinegar
- ½ cup ketchup
- 3 Tbsp. Worcestershire sauce
- 1 tsp. garlic salt
- 3 Tbsp. chopped onion
- 2 Tbsp. brown sugar
- ¼–½ tsp. pepper

Instructions:

1. Place the turkey cutlets in a slow baking oven.

2. In a cup, combine the remaining ingredients. Pour the turkey on.

3. Cover. Cook for less than 4 hours. Serve over rice, either white or brown. A great variation —

3.30. Turkey Salad

(Serves 8, Cook Time 1 Hour 10 Minutes, Difficulty: Normal)

Ingredients:

- 4 cups cooked, cubed turkey
- 4 cups celery, chopped (get out your food processor)
- 1 cup blanched almonds, chopped
- ¾ cup chopped green bell pepper

- ¼ cup chopped pimento
- ¼ cup chopped onion
- 2 tsp. salt
- ¼ cup lemon juice 1 cup mayonnaise
- 8 oz. Swiss cheese, sliced
- 8 oz. Swiss cheese, sliced
- 1 stick (½ cup) butter, melted
- 2 cups cracker crumbs

Instructions:

1. If you don't have cooked turkey (or chicken), flip to page 360 for a recipe for cooking poultry in your slow cooker, so you have it ready for recipes like this one. If you've got the cooked turkey already, go ahead with Step 2.

2. In a big bowl, gently mix the turkey, celery, almonds, green pepper, pimentos, onion, salt, lemon juice, and mayonnaise.

3. Spoon the mixture into your greased slow cooker. Top with slices of cheese.

4. Cover. Cook on Low 2½–3 hours, or until the celery, pepper, and onions are as tender as you like them.

5. While the turkey is cooking, combine the melted butter and cracker crumbs in a small bowl.

6. When the turkey is finished cooking, sprinkle the buttered cracker crumbs over the top.

7. Continue cooking, uncovered, for 15 minutes, or until the topping is heated through.

3.31. Turkey Enchiladas

(Serves 6, Cook Time 2-3 Hours, Difficulty: Hard)

Ingredients:

- 1 large onion, chopped

- 2 Tbsp. olive oil
- ¼ tsp. garlic powder
- 1 tsp. salt
- ½ tsp. dried oregano
- 2 4-oz. cans diced green chilies
- 28-oz. can stew tomatoes
- 6 corn, or flour, tortillas, divided
- 2 cups chopped, cooked turkey
- 1 cup sour cream, plus more for passing as a topping
- 2 cups grated cheddar cheese, plus more for passing as a topping fresh cilantro, chopped, for

Instructions:

1. Sauté the onion in the olive oil in a good-sized skillet. When the onion softens, stir in the garlic powder, salt, and oregano. Give the mixture a swirl, and then take it off the heat.

2. Stir in the chilies and tomatoes.

3. Lay 2-tortillas into the bottom of your greased slow cooker. Tear them so that they cover the bottom of the cooker as much as possible.

4. Ladle in ⅓ of the tomato mixture.

5. Mix the turkey, 1 cup sour cream, and 2 cups grated cheese together in a bowl—spoon ⅓ of that mixture over the tomato sauce.

6. Repeat the layers twice. 7. Cover. Cook on Low 4–6 hours.

8. Let the Enchiladas stand for 15 minutes before serving to let the cheese firm up.

9. Serve with toppings of more sour cream, more grated cheese, and fresh cilantro.

3.32. Mustard-Glazed Tomatoes

(Serves 2, Cook Time 30 Minutes, Difficulty: Normal)

Ingredients:

- 4 large tomatoes
- 1/2 tsp. salt
- 1/2 tsp. dried thyme
- 2 tbsp. brown sugar
- 2 tbsp. Dijon mustard
- 2 tbsp. butter

Instructions:

1. Crop a thin slice from the edge within each tomato. Using a small knife, make a cross-cut on each tomato's top about 1 inch long.

2. For the tomato cut-side up, add a small foil baking bowl. Stir together the flour, thyme, sugar, and mustard; spread the mixture thinly on top of the tomatoes.

3. A dot, each with butter. Bake on a burner or directly on a grill for about 20-minutes or until the tomatoes are softened and cooked.

3.33. Campfire Chili

(Serves 4, Cook Time 30 Minutes, Difficulty: Normal)

Ingredients:

- 1 lb. ground beef
- 1/2 large onion, chopped
- 2 garlic cloves, minced
- 1 bell pepper, chopped
- 1 can (8 oz.) kidney beans, drained

- 2 cans (19 oz.) tomato sauce
- Chili powder
- Salt and black pepper
- Cumin

Instructions:

1. Drain the kidney beans and apply the tomato sauce. Store in a jar with tight sealing.

2. Chop the onion, bell pepper and garlic; mix and store until ready to use in the refrigerator or cooler.

3.34. Shredded Baked Potatoes

(Serves 4-6, Cook Time 55 Minutes, Difficulty: Normal)

Ingredients:

- 4 large cooked baking potatoes
- 1 1/2 cup sour cream
- 1 cup Cheddar cheese, shredded
- 4 green onions, chopped
- 1/2 tsp. salt and pepper

Instructions:

1. In a large saucepan, prepare the potatoes till they are fork ready.

2. Grate or dice thinly until cold enough for sour cream, melted cheese, onions, salt, and pepper to blend and whisk in. For better safety, spoon on a large sheet of foil, cover and refrigerate the sides for up to one day, or freeze.

3. In the camp: thaw potatoes, if frozen, and place them in an oven in the Netherlands. Cook over medium-hot heat or when thoroughly cooked, for 30 minutes.

3.35. Grilled Portobello Mushrooms

(Serves 4, Cook Time 17 Minutes, Difficulty: Normal)

Ingredients

- 4 large Portobello mushrooms
- 2 tbsp. balsamic vinegar
- 1 tsp. garlic
- 1 tsp. dried basil
- Salt and pepper to taste
- Olive oil

Instructions:

1. Pour the combination of vinegar over the mushrooms and leave to marinate for 30 minutes. Mushrooms should be removed and marinade reserved. Place the mushrooms on a finely oiled grill rack if you use a grill.

2. Cover the lid and cook for 7 minutes or until the mushrooms are golden brown and hot; brush with the vinegar mixture periodically—season with salt and pepper to taste. Place mushrooms in the grill basket when open-fire cooking, cook over low embers until mushrooms are golden brown; turn basket regularly for even cooking.

3. You can also put mushrooms inside a foil packet with a little bit of the mixture and encourage them to cook over an open flame.

3.36. Greek Potatoes

(Serves 4-6, Cook Time 30 Minutes, Difficulty: Normal)

Ingredients:

- 1/4 cup water
- 3 tbsp. olive oil
- 2 cloves garlic, minced

- 1 tsp. dried rosemary
- 5 medium red or white potatoes, peeled and sliced lengthwise into thick slices
- 1/4 cup crumbled feta cheese
- Lemon juice
- Zest from 1 lemon
- Salt and pepper

Instructions:

1. In a wide plastic bag or cup, mix the lemon juice, zest, water, oil, garlic, and rosemary.

2. Add the potatoes to coat, and toss. Spread the potato mixture in one layer, including the liquid, on a large sheet of heavy-duty foil. Cover with the feta cheese and brush lightly with salt and pepper.

3. Fold the ends of the foil together to create a secure seal that forms a box. Place the packet in a Dutch oven and cook for 25 minutes over medium-hot heat or until the potatoes are tender, turning golden brown.

4. Remove from the heat and allow to stay until the foil is cool enough to treat.

3.37. Hobo Chicken and Vegetables

(Serves 4, Cook Time 1 Hour 10 Minutes, Difficulty: Normal)

Ingredients:

- 1 lb. chicken breast, skinless, boneless, cubed
- 1 onion, diced
- 1 pkg (8 oz.) mushrooms
- 4 cloves garlic, diced
- 4 small potatoes, cubed
- 1/4 cup butter

- 1 lemon, juiced

Instructions:

1. In a wide bowl or zip-lock bag, combine the chicken, onion, mushrooms, garlic, and potatoes. Apply the lemon juice, then mix well. Divide the mixture into four wide aluminum foil pieces evenly, place the mixture in the middle and cover with butter slices.

2. Fold the foil's two ends to meet in the middle and roll downwards to seal them. The remaining two ends roll inwards into the mixture so that it is reliable.

3. Place over a campfire with the seam side up for approximately 40 minutes or until the chicken is thoroughly cooked. Remove from the fire and allow to cool for a couple of minutes. Be very careful about opening foil pouches so that the steam does not fry you.

3.38. Grilled Salmon with Lemon

(Serves 4, Cook Time 20 Minutes, Difficulty: Normal)

Ingredients:

- 1/2 cup fresh lemon juice
- 1/4 cup olive oil
- 1 small onion, finely chopped
- 1 clove garlic, minced
- 2 tsp. dried dill
- Salmon
- Salt and black pepper to taste

Instructions:

1. Lemon juice, oil, onion, garlic, dill salt, and pepper are mixed at home. Store in a securely packed bag and store until ready for use in the refrigerator or cooler. For more extended storage, freeze.

2. At Camp: Thaw, if frozen, marinade. Put the salmon and pour the marinade over the salmon in a shallow pan and let stand for 20 minutes before frying.

3. Take the fish out and discard the marinade. Place on a grill rack with fish skin-side down.

4. Cook for 10 minutes per inch of thickness over medium-hot heat, or until the fish is opaque and flakes easily with a fork.

3.39. Hawaiian Style Pork Chops

(Serves 4, Cook Time 22 Minutes, Difficulty: Normal)

Ingredients:

- 1 cup pineapple juice
- 1 small onion, diced
- 3 tbsp. soy sauce
- 2 tbsp. brown sugar
- 1 tbsp. sesame oil
- Boned pork chops
- Salt and black pepper to taste

Instructions:

1. The marinade chops are cut and the marinade is poured.

2. Cook over medium-hot sun on a finely oiled grill rack, rotating once, for 5 min per side or until an instant read thermometer inserted into the center of the chops reads 170 ° F.

3.40. Herb-Stuffed Grilled Fish

(Serves 4, Cook Time 22 Minutes, Difficulty: Normal)

Ingredients:

- 2 tbsp. olive oil
- Zest from 1 lime
- 4 fresh dill branches
- 4 green onions

- Canola oil
- 1 small clove garlic, crushed
- 2 fresh fish fillets
- Lime juice
- Salt and pepper to taste

Instructions:

1. Sauce with the lime thaw, if frozen. Pat the dried fish fillets with paper towels. It is crucial to place green onions and dills along the length of one fish fillet.

2. Use a second fillet to cover; gently brush the fish with grease.

3. Wrap up in foil, comfortably protected. Cook over medium-hot heat or on a finely oiled grill rack for 10 minutes or until the fish is opaque and fork-flaked easily. To taste, season with salt and pepper. Serve with cod drizzled with lime-sauce.

3.41. Margarita Pizza with Beer Crust

(Serves 4, Cook Time 40 Minutes, Difficulty: Normal)

Ingredients:

Crust:

- 3 cup all-purpose flour
- 1 tbsp. baking powder
- 1/2 tsp. salt
- 1/2 dried oregano or basil
- 1 12 oz. can beer

Pizza Filling:

- 4 medium tomatoes, chopped
- 2 cup mozzarella cheese, shredded

- 1/4 cup Parmesan cheese, shredded
- 1 tbsp. dried basil
- 1 tbsp. dried oregano
- 2 cloves garlic, finely diced
- Salt and pepper to taste

Toppings:

- Pepperoni
- Bell pepper, chopped
- Mushrooms
- Olives
- Onion, chopped
- Hamburger
- Pineapple

Instructions:

1. In a wide tub, combine the flour mixture with the beer and stir gently until combined. On a flat, gently floured board, transform the dough and knead it several times.

2. Brush the dough generously with oil, cover with sliced tomatoes and basil, sprinkle thinly with the cheeses, and add the appropriate toppings to the edge of each plate. In two pizza pans, pat the dough.

3. Bake on a grill rack or Coleman stove on the moderate flame until the dough is thoroughly cooked.

4. Slice as wedges and serve.

3.42. Pan-Fried Potatoes and Mushrooms

(Serves 2, Cook Time 25 Minutes, Difficulty: Normal)

Ingredients:

- 1 small onion, chopped
- 2 tbsp. butter
- 2 cup potatoes, cooked and diced
- 1/2 cup mushrooms
- 1 cup cheddar cheese, shredded
- Salt and black pepper to taste

Instructions:

1. In a medium skillet over medium flame, sauté the onion in the butter for 5 minutes or until tender. Combine the potatoes and mushrooms and finish cooking for 5 minutes.

2. For an additional 5 minutes, add seasonings, scatter with cheese, relieve friction, cover, and boil until the cheese is melted. Serve instantly.

3.43. Slow-Cooked Pulled Pork

(Serves 2, Cook Time 25 Minutes, Difficulty: Normal)

Ingredients:

- 1 cup chili sauce
- 1/3 cup Dijon mustard
- 1/3 cup honey
- 2 tbsp. chili powder
- 2 tbsp. tomato paste
- 2 tbsp. Worcestershire sauce
- 1 tbsp. packed brown sugar

- 2 tsp. paprika
- 2 large clove garlic, minced
- 2 cup sliced onion
- 3-4 lbs. pork shoulder roast
- 2 cup chopped apples
- Large ciabatta rolls, onion buns

Instructions:

1. Mix the hot sauce, vinegar, butter, chili powder, tomato paste, Worcestershire sauce, brown sugar, paprika, and garlic at home. Place or freeze in a closely sealed jar for more extended storage.

2. At Camp: Thaw, if frozen, sauce. Place the onions in the lower section of the Dutch oven. Place the pork over the onions and apples on top. Pour the sauce over the apples and beef.

3. Cover and simmer for 4 hours over medium heat or until the meat is tender and starting to fall apart. Take the meat from the oven and use forks to shred the meat. Serve with rolls as a garnish using the leftover sauce.

3.44. Caprese Chicken Skewers

(Serves 4, Cook Time 15 Minutes, Difficulty: Normal)

Ingredients:

- 1-pound chicken breasts
- 12 cherry tomatoes
- 8 Mozzarella cheese balls, halved
- 4 basil leaves, roughly chopped
- 1 teaspoon oregano
- ½ teaspoon salt

- ½ teaspoon black pepper
- Extra virgin olive oil

Instructions:

1. Slice chicken into cubes.

2. Mix all the seasonings and add chicken.

3. Divide into skewers, and when cooked, add cheese balls on both sides of skewers.

3.45. Chicken Bacon Tootsies

(Serves 4, Cook Time 10 Minutes, Difficulty: Normal)

Ingredients

- 4 medium chicken breasts
- 12 sliced bacon
- Vegetable oil

Instructions:

1. Slice the chicken breasts into 1.5 bits and divide them into four sticks.

2. Around each skewer, wrap three bacon slices and grill over the fire for about 7 minutes.

3. Start serving with a good salad, green, or Caesar.

3.46. Cajun Chicken Breast Sandwiches

(Serves 4, Cook Time 15 Minutes, Difficulty: Normal)

Ingredients:

- 4 chicken boneless breasts
- 2 teaspoons Cajun spice
- ¼ cup hot sauce
- 4 slices cheddar cheese

- Lettuce 1 onion
- Sliced 4 crusty buns

Instructions:

1. Pound chicken breasts into 1/2 thickness.

2. Heat and grease the grill, put the chicken breast, and cook for 8 minutes.

3. Add Cajun spice and hot sauce to the chicken.

5. Warms the buns and add chicken mince into it.

3.47. Spit-Fire Chicken

(Serves 4, Cook Time 15 Minutes, Difficulty: Normal)

Ingredients:

- 1 whole chicken, about 4 pounds
- 1 teaspoon cumin
- 1 teaspoon salt
- 1 teaspoon black pepper
- ½ teaspoon rosemary
- ¼ teaspoon cinnamon

Instructions:

1. On spit roasting sticks, cook chicken mixed in spices until tender.

3.48. Turkey Pimento Burgers

(Serves 4, Cook Time 15 Minutes, Difficulty: Normal)

Ingredients:

- 1½ pounds ground turkey.
- 2 pimento peppers,

- Minced 4 slices old cheddar cheese.
- 4 tablespoons mayonnaise.
- ½ teaspoon salt
- ½ teaspoon black pepper
- 4 hamburger buns
- Vegetable oil

Topping:

- 1 tomato,
- Sliced lettuce,
- Chopped tomato ketchup
- Mustard

Instructions:

1. You will need to prepare this marinade ahead of time because you need to use a blender.

2. Combine all the ingredients except the chicken in a blender and whisk until relatively smooth.

3. In a freezer bag, put the marinade and chicken legs, and then marinate for up to 12 hours before departing for your trip.

4. Heat the grill to medium-high, coat the chicken with vegetable oil, and roast the chicken legs for about 25 minutes.

5. Serve with rice or a pasta salad.

3.49. Jerk Chicken Legs

(Serves 4, Cook Time 35 Minutes, Difficulty: Normal)

Ingredients:

- 4 chicken legs with thighs
- 1 Habanero chili pepper, trimmed and sliced
- 1 onion 1 scallion 2 garlic cloves
- ⅓ cup soy sauce
- 1 teaspoon 5 spice powder
- ¼ teaspoon nutmeg
- ¼ teaspoon cinnamon
- 1 teaspoon salt

Instructions:

1. You will need to prepare this marinade ahead of time because you need to use a blender.

2. Combine all the ingredients except the chicken in a blender and whisk until relatively smooth.

3. In a freezer bag, put the marinade and chicken legs, and then marinate for up to 12 hours before departing for your trip.

4. Heat the grill to medium-high, coat the chicken with vegetable oil, and roast the chicken legs for about 25 minutes.

5. Serve with rice or a pasta salad.

3.50. Beer Chicken and Fingerling Potatoes

(Serves 4, Cook Time 35 Minutes, Difficulty: Normal)

Ingredients:

- 8 chicken thighs
- 1 can dark beer
- ½ cup BBQ sauce
- 20 fingerling potatoes
- 1 teaspoon rosemary
- 1 teaspoon salt
- 1 teaspoon black pepper
- Vegetable oil

Instructions:

1. Combine 1/2 teaspoon of salt, 1/2 teaspoon of black pepper, 1/2 teaspoon of salt, BBQ sauce, and beer. Add half a teaspoon of paprika to a dish, add the chicken thighs, and add the chicken thighs. For an hour, marinate.

2. Combine 3-teaspoons of vegetable oil and 1/2 teaspoon of salt with a rosemary teaspoon and combine well.

3. To add to the oil mixture, cut the potatoes in half and set them aside.

4. Wait for the flames to die and the hot coals to remain—light up the fuel.

5. Cover a griddle with vegetable oil.

6. Place the chicken and the potatoes on the barbecue.

7. Cook for 25 minutes, then switch on the chicken and potatoes after the first 10 minutes.

Chapter 4: Camping Breakfast Recipes

In this chapter, we will provide you Breakfast Recipes that you can cook while camping.

4.1. Muffin Tin Bacon N Eggs

(Serves 4, Cook Time 10 Minutes, Difficulty: Normal)

Ingredients:

- 3 slices of bacon
- 6 eggs

Instructions:

1. Cut bacon slices into fourths.

2. In a muffin tin, place two pieces of bacon in the bottom of each cup in the shape of an 'X.'

3. Place over medium heat for 2-3 minutes.

4. Remove from heat and flip bacon over so that the uncooked side is down. Crack an egg in each cup on top of semi-cooked bacon and place over medium heat for another 2-3 minutes or until eggs are cooked as desired.

5. Using a fork, remove from tin onto a plate, and enjoy.

4.2. Berry Pancakes

(Serves 8, Cook Time 10-20 Minutes, Difficulty: Normal)

Ingredients:

- 3/4 c oat or wheat bran
- 1/2 c whole wheat flour
- 1/4 c ground flaxseed
- 1 tbsp baking powder
- 1 tbsp granulated sugar
- 1 c milk
- 1 tsp canola oil
- 1 egg, beaten
- 1 c blueberries
- Pinch of salt
- Oil or nonstick cooking spray

Ingredients:

1. Place dry ingredients in a medium bowl.

2. In a second bowl, combine milk, oil, and egg. Add wet ingredients to dry ingredients and stir until blended; fold in the berries.

3. Heat a well-oiled pan over medium heat until hot. Drop batter by the spoonful onto the pan. Cook pancakes for 3 min or until bubbles break on top and the underside is golden brown; turn and cook the second side until golden.

4. Serve with maple syrup or powdered sugar.

4.3. Granola Bread

(Serves 4, Cook Time 30 Minutes, Difficulty: Normal)

Ingredients:

- 1 3/4 c all-purpose flour
- 1 tsp baking powder
- 1 tsp baking soda
- 1/2 tsp ground nutmeg
- 1/2 tsp cinnamon pinch salt
- 1 c plain yogurt
- 1 egg
- 2 tsp vanilla extract
- 1 c sugar
- 1/4 c butter, softened
- 2/3 c family-style granola

Ingredients:

1. In a large bowl, cream the sugar with butter; add the yogurt mixture and stir until creamy. Stir in dry ingredients and spoon into a greased 8-inch metal baking pan. Sprinkle with granola.

2. Place pan in a Dutch oven. Bake for 35 minutes at 350°F or until cake springs back when lightly touched. Cool before serving.

4.4. Grilled Banana Oatmeal Pancakes

(Serves 14, Cook Time 20 Minutes, Difficulty: Normal)

Ingredients:

- 1 c large flaked rolled oats

- 1 c whole wheat flour
- 1/4 c lightly packed brown sugar
- 1 tsp baking powder
- 1 tsp baking soda
- 1/4 tsp salt
- 1/4 tsp ground cinnamon
- 1 ripe banana, mashed
- 2 eggs, beaten
- 1 c plain yogurt
- 1/2 c milk
- 1/4 c canola oil
- 1 tsp vanilla extract
- Non-stick cooking spray

Ingredients:

1. Stir banana mixture into dry ingredients until blended.

2. Heat a large skillet over medium heat and spray with non-stick cooking spray. Drop batter, by the large spoonful, onto the pan.

3. Cook pancakes for 3 minutes or until bubbles break on the surface and the underside is golden brown; turn and cook the second side for 3 minutes or until golden brown.

4. Serve with syrup, powdered sugar, peanut butter, or eat plain

4.5. Eggs Benedict

(Serves 2-4, Cook Time 20 Minutes, Difficulty: Normal)

Ingredients:

- 1/4 c light mayonnaise

- 2 tbsp plain yogurt
- 1 tbsp Dijon mustard
- 1-2 tsp fresh lemon juice
- 4 eggs
- 4 bacon slices, halved
- 2 English muffins, halved and toasted
- 1 tbsp butter
- Ground black pepper

Instructions:

1. In a small bowl, stir together the mayonnaise, yogurt, mustard, and lemon juice. In a medium non-stick skillet, add 1 inch of water; bring to a gentle boil.

2. Slowly slide eggs into the water and poach eggs for 3 minutes or until cooked as desired. Remove from water and place on a warm plate to drain.

3. Cook bacon as desired. Place muffin halves on plates and spread with butter. Top with one egg, two half slices of bacon, and spoon sauce over the top.

4. Season with pepper as desired.

4.6. Camp-Style Chocolate Pitas

(Serves 2, Cook Time 15 Minutes, Difficulty: Normal)

Ingredients:

- 2 pieces pita bread, cut in half
- Dark chocolate squares or handful of chocolate chips

Instructions:

1. Over moderate heat, heat a non-stick skillet.

2. Add several chocolate squares into the pitas' open hand.

3. Grill the pitas on each hand for 2 minutes or before the chocolate melts.

4.7. Cinnamon French toast

(Serves 2-4, Cook Time 20 Minutes, Difficulty: Normal)

Ingredients:

- 3 eggs
- 1/3 c milk
- 1 tsp ground cinnamon
- 8 slices bread
- Oil or nonstick cooking spray

Instructions:

1. Heat a well-oiled pan on medium heat.

2. In a shallow dish, whisk together eggs, milk, and cinnamon.

3. Dip bread slices in egg mixture, turning each slice to coat well.

4. Place as many slices in the pan as possible—Cook over medium heat for 2 min. Turn and cook the second side for 2 min or until golden brown. Serve with syrup or powdered sugar.

4.8. Camp Granola

(Serves 5, Cook Time 40 Minutes, Difficulty: Normal)

Ingredients:

- 3 c old fashioned rolled oats
- 1 c coarsely chopped pecans
- 1/2 c unsweetened coconut
- 2 tbsp packed brown sugar
- 1/2 tsp ground cinnamon

- 1/4 tsp ground allspice
- 1/4 tsp nutmeg
- Pinch salt
- 1/3 c honey
- 2 tbsp canola oil
- 1 c assorted dried fruit
- 1/4 c sunflower seeds
- 1/4 c sliced almonds
- 1/4 c sesame seeds

Instructions:

1. In a large bowl, combine rolled oats, nuts, coconut, sunflower and sesame seeds, sugar, spices, and salt.

2. In a small bowl, stir together the honey and oil; pour over the oat mixture stirring well to distribute. Spoon mixture onto a large parchment-lined baking sheet and bake at 300° F for about 40 min; stir every 10 min. Remove from oven and stir in dried fruit.

3. When cool, store in a tightly sealed container for up to 1 month.

4.9. Granola Bars

(Serves 12, Cook Time 30 Minutes, Difficulty: Normal)

Ingredients:

- 1/2 c corn syrup
- 2 tbsp packed brown sugar
- 1/3 c crunchy peanut butter
- 3 1/2 c granola
- 1/4 c ground flaxseed

- 1 tsp ground allspice or cinnamon

Instructions:

1. In a large microwave-safe container, combine syrup and sugar.

2. Cook on high for 1 1/2 min or until mixture is boiling; stir in peanut butter until smooth.

3. Quickly stir in granola, flaxseed, and allspice until the mixture is well combined.

4. Spoon into a lightly greased 8. metal pan; press down firmly.

5. Allow cooling before cutting into slices. Store in a tightly sealed container.

4.10. Fruity Fiber Cookies

(Serves 30, Cook Time 55 Minutes, Difficulty: Normal)

Ingredients:

- 4 medium bananas
- 1/3 c canola oil
- 1 1/2 c rolled oats
- 3/4 c whole wheat flour
- 1/2 c dried raisins
- 1/2 c apricots, chopped
- 1 1/2 c dates
- 1/2 c chopped pecans, walnuts or almonds

Instructions:

1. In a large bowl, mash bananas. Combine bananas with oil, oats, flour, raisins, apricots, dates, and nuts; mix well.

2. Drop by spoonful onto a greased baking sheet; flatten with a fork. Bake cookies at 350°F for 20 min or until cookies are golden brown.

3. Cool completely before storing in a tightly sealed container.

4. You may freeze for more extended storage.

4.11. Mini Frittatas

(Serves 2, Cook Time 10 Minutes, Difficulty: Normal)

Ingredients:

- 4 eggs
- 1/4 c half and half
- 1/2 tsp salt
- Grated cheese
- Diced onions and green peppers
- Chopped bacon, ham or sausage
- Non-stick cooking spray

Instructions:

1. In a small bowl, mix eggs, half and half, and salt. In a muffin tin, evenly distribute the egg mixture into each cup.

2. Add onions, peppers, cheese, and meat to each cup as desired.

3. Place muffin tin over medium heat for 5 minutes or until eggs are done as desired.

4. Use a knife to loosen around the edges before removing from muffin tin.

4.12. Hot Multigrain Cereal

(Serves 4, Cook Time 10 Minutes, Difficulty: Easy)

Ingredients:

- 1 c rolled oats
- 1 c seven- grain cereal
- 1 c whole wheat flakes
- 1 c oat bran

- 1 c ground flaxseed or wheat germ

Instructions:

1. In a saucepan, bring 1/4 c cereal and ¾ c water to a boil, reduce heat to medium-low and allow to cook for another 5 minutes, stirring constantly, until cereal reaches desired consistency.

2. Cover and remove from heat and let stand for a few min before serving.

4.13. Breakfast Burritos

(Serves 4-6, Cook Time 20 Minutes, Difficulty: Normal)

Ingredients:

- 6 eggs
- 1/2 c milk or water
- 1 small onion, chopped
- 1 tbsp butter
- 1/2 c grated cheese
- 6 large tortillas
- Salsa or picante
- Salt and ground black pepper

Instructions:

1. In a bowl, combine eggs, milk, salt, and pepper.

2. In a non-stick skillet, cook onion in butter for 5 min.

3. Add egg mixture and cook over medium heat, stirring occasionally. Add cheese just before eggs are set.

4. Warm tortillas by the fire, place on a flat surface, and fill each with some of the egg mixtures. Roll up and serve with salsa.

4.14. Overnight Cheese Casserole

(Serves 4, Cook Time 35 Minutes, Difficulty: Normal)

Ingredients:

- 6 slices bread
- 3 c grated cheese
- 6 eggs, beaten
- 2 c milk
- 1/2 medium onion, chopped
- 1 sun-dried tomato, diced
- Salt and ground black pepper

Instructions:

1. Arrange bread slices in a greased metal baking pan that will hold six slices. Sprinkle with half of the cheese.

2. In a bowl, combine eggs, milk, onion, and tomato. Pour over bread. Sprinkle with remaining cheese, salt, and pepper.

3. Cover and store in a cooler overnight. Bake in a Dutch oven at 350°F for about 35 minutes or until browned.

4. Let sit for 5 min before cutting into squares.

4.15. Muffin Tin Bacon and Eggs

(Serves 2, Cook Time 10 Minutes, Difficulty: Easy)

Ingredients:

- 1 bowl Bacon
- 4 Eggs
- Salt to taste

Instructions:

1. Heat the bacon in muffin cups for 2 minutes

2. Crack and add egg, sprinkle salt.

3. Cook for 6 to 7 minutes on low flame

4. Serve hot.

4.16. Berry Pancakes

(Serves 8, Cook Time 15 Minutes, Difficulty: Easy)

Ingredients:

- 3/4 cup oat or wheat bran
- 1/2 cup whole wheat flour
- 1/4 cup ground flaxseed
- 1 tbsp. baking powder
- 1 tbsp. granulated sugar
- 1 cup milk
- 1 tsp. canola oil
- 1 egg, beaten
- 1 cup blueberries
- Pinch of salt
- Oil or nonstick cooking spray

Instructions:

1. Mix dry ingredients in one bowl and wet in another.

2. Grease and heat pan

3. Add batter and cook for 10 min

4. Let it cool for 3 or 4 min and serve.

4.17. Grilled Banana Oatmeal Pancakes

(Serves 2, Cook Time 20 Minutes, Difficulty: Normal)

Ingredients:

- Flaked rolled oats 1 large cup ¼ Cup brown sugar
- 1 cup whole wheat flour
- 1/4 cup lightly packed brown sugar
- One tsp. Baking powder
- 1 tsp. Baking soda
- 1/4 tsp. Salt
- 1/4 tsp. Ground cinnamon
- 1 ripe banana, mashed
- 2 eggs, beaten
- 1 cup plain yogurt
- 1/2 cup milk
- 1/4 cup canola oil
- 1 tsp. vanilla extract nonstick cooking spray

Instructions:

1. Mix bananas in dry ingredients and wet ingredients
2. Oil and heat the pan
3. Cook on a medium flame for 5 or 6 minutes
4. Serve hot.

4.18. Eggs Benedict

(Serves 2, Cook Time 12 Minutes, Difficulty: Normal)

Ingredients:

For Sauce:

- 1/4 cup light mayonnaise
- 2 tbsp. plain yogurt
- 1 tbsp. Dijon mustard
- 1-2 tsp. fresh lemon juice

The benedict:

- 4 eggs
- 4 bacon slices, halved
- 2 English muffins, halved and toasted
- 1 tbsp. butter
- Ground black pepper

Instructions:

1. Mix sauce ingredients, bring to boil
2. Cook bacon, poach eggs in water.
3. Place muffin halves on bacon, top it with one egg and drizzle sauce.
4. Serve hot.

4.19. Camp-Style Chocolate Pitas

(Serves 2, Cook Time 15 Minutes, Difficulty: Normal)

Ingredients:

- 2 pieces pita bread, cut in half

- Dark chocolate squares or a handful of chocolate chips

Instructions:

1. Heat the skillet

2. Insert the chocolate in open spaces of bread

3. Cook till the chocolate melts

4.20. Cinnamon French toast

(Serves 2, Cook Time 15 Minutes, Difficulty: Normal)

Ingredients:

- 3 eggs
- 1/3 cup milk
- 1 tsp. ground cinnamon
- 8 slices bread
- Oil or nonstick cooking spray

Instructions:

1. Mix wet ingredients

2. Heat the pan with oil

3. Dip the slices

4. Fry till golden brown.

4.21. Camp Granola

(Serves 2, Cook Time 40 Minutes, Difficulty: Normal)

Ingredients:

- 3 cup old fashioned rolled oats
- 1 cup coarsely chopped pecans

- 1/2 cup unsweetened coconut
- 2 tbsp. packed brown sugar
- 1/2 tsp. ground cinnamon
- 1/4 tsp. ground allspice
- 1/4 tsp. nutmeg
- Pinch salt
- 1/3 cup honey
- 2 tbsp. canola oil
- 1 cup assorted dried fruit
- 1/4 cup sunflower seeds
- 1/4 cup sliced almonds
- 1/4 cup sesame seeds

Instructions:

1. Mix all the wet and dry ingredients.

2. Spread on a parchment-lined baking sheet.

3. Bake at 300° F for 40 minutes, stir every 10 minutes.

4. When cool, store in a dry place for 1 month.

4.22. Granola Bars

(Serves 5, Cook Time 15 Minutes, Difficulty: Normal)

Ingredients:

- 1/2 cup corn syrup
- 2 tbsp. packed brown sugar
- 1/3 cup crunchy peanut butter
- 3 1/2 cup granola

- 1/4 cup ground flaxseed
- 1 tsp. ground allspice or cinnamon

Instructions:

1. Boil sugar in water for 2 3 minutes

2. Add in peanut butter, mix well

3. Mix all the dry ingredients and add to the liquid mix.

4. Dish out in a greased pan, press with a spoon, and flatten.

5. Cut in slices when cool.

4.23. Fruity Fiber Cookies

(Serves 2, Cook Time 35 Minutes, Difficulty: Normal)

Ingredients:

- 4 medium bananas
- 1/3 cup canola oil
- 1 1/2 cup rolled oats
- 3/4 cup whole wheat flour
- 1/2 cup dried raisins
- 1/2 cup apricots, chopped
- 1 1/2 cup dates
- 1/2 c chopped pecans, walnuts or almonds

Instructions:

1. In a large bowl, mash bananas, add all the ingredients and mix well.

2. Spoon out on a greased pan, flatten, and bake at 350°F for 20 minutes.

3. Serve when cool.

4.24. Mini Frittatas

(Serves 4, Cook Time 10 Minutes, Difficulty: Normal)

Ingredients:

- 4 eggs
- 1/4 cup half and half
- 1/2 tsp. salt
- Grated cheese
- Diced onions and green peppers
- Chopped bacon, ham or sausage
- Nonstick cooking spray

Instructions:

1. Mix eggs in a bowl and add salt.

2. Pour into muffin tin, add on vegetables and meat.

3. Place on medium heat until done.

4.25. Peanut Butter Banana Muffins

(Serves 12, Cook Time 28 Minutes, Difficulty: Normal)

Ingredients:

- 1 1/4 cup all-purpose flour
- 1/2 cup whole wheat flour
- 2/3 cup brown sugar
- 2 tsp. baking powder
- 1tsp ground cinnamon
- 1/2 tsp. baking soda
- 1/2 tsp. salt

- 2 large bananas, mashed
- 1/2 cup butter, softened
- 1/3 cup peanut butter
- 2 eggs, beaten
- 1 tsp. vanilla extract

Instructions:

1. Mix all the ingredients well.

2. Dish out in a muffin dish lined with baking cups.

3. Bake at 375°F for 10 minutes or until done.

4.26. Hot Multigrain Cereal

(Serves 4, Cook Time 15 Minutes, Difficulty: Normal)

Ingredients:

- 1 cup rolled oats
- 1 cup seven-grain cereal
- 1 cup whole wheat flakes
- 1 cup oat bran
- 1 cup ground flaxseed or wheat germ

Instructions:

1. In a saucepan, mix ¼ cup cereal and ¾ cup water and boil.

2. Reduce heat to medium-low and cook for another 5 minutes, continually stirring, until cereal reaches desired consistency.

4.27. Breakfast Burritos

(Serves 4, Cook Time 20 Minutes, Difficulty: Normal)

Ingredients:

- 6 eggs
- 1/2 cup milk or water
- 1 small onion, chopped
- 1 tbsp. butter
- 1/2 cup grated cheese
- 6 large tortillas
- Salsa or Picante
- Salt and ground black pepper

Instructions:

1. Mix eggs, salt and pepper in one bowl.

2. Cook on medium flame on a greased pan.

3. Add cheese after the eggs set.

4. Warm tortillas on flame, fill with the egg mix and roll.

5. Serve hot with salsa.

4.28. Overnight Cheese Casserole

(Serves 4, Cook Time 50 Minutes, Difficulty: Normal)

Ingredients:

- 6 slices bread
- 3 c grated cheese
- 6 eggs, beaten
- 2 c milk
- 1/2 medium onion, chopped
- 1 sun-dried tomato, diced
- Salt and ground black pepper

Instructions:

1. Spread slices on a baking pan and cover with cheese, add the egg mix and then add the remaining cheese.

2. Keep it covered in a cooler.

3. Bake it in a Dutch oven the next morning at 350°F for 35 minutes.

4. Let it cool for 5 minutes and then cut into slices.

4.29. Potato Subs (Indian)

(Serves 4, Cook Time 40 Minutes, Difficulty: Normal)

Ingredients:

- Potatoes 1.5 cup
- Tomatoes half cup
- Onions half cup
- Salt
- Red Chili powder half tsp.
- 1/3 tsp. Coriander powder
- 1 green chili
- Half tsp. Ginger Garlic paste
- 3 tbsp. Oil

Instructions:

1. Heat the pan and oil, mix all the ingredients.

2. Cover and cook for some 25 minutes.

3. Garnish with green chili. Serve with the tortilla.

4.30. Fruit Mix

(Serves 2, Cook Time 20 Minutes, Difficulty: Normal)

Ingredients:

- 4 bananas
- 1 apple
- A bunch of grapes
- 1 peach
- Salt
- Pepper
- 1 tsp. Sugar
- Any other seasonal fruit

Instructions:

1. Cut the apple, bananas and peach.
2. Add on the grapes or any other seasonal fruit.
3. Add salt, pepper and sugar. Mix well.

4.31. Peanut Butter Banana

(Serves 12, Cook Time 15 Minutes, Difficulty: Normal)

Ingredients:

- 1 1/4 c all-purpose flour
- 1/2 c whole wheat flour
- 2/3 c brown sugar
- 2 tsp baking powder
- 1tsp ground cinnamon

- 1/2 tsp baking soda
- 1/2 tsp salt
- 2 large bananas, mashed
- 1/2 c butter, softened
- 1/3 c peanut butter
- 2 eggs, beaten
- 1 tsp vanilla extract

Instructions:

1. In a large bowl, combine flours, sugar, baking powder, cinnamon, baking soda and salt.

2. In a second bowl, combine mashed bananas, butter, peanut butter, eggs and vanilla; stir into flour mixture until thoroughly mixed. Spoon batter into nonstick or paper lined muffin cups, filling 2/3rds full.

3. Bake at 375°F for 18 min or until muffins are lightly browned and firm to the touch. Cool for 10 min before removing to a wire rack to cool completely. Pack in an airtight bag and freeze until needed.

Chapter 5: Camping Midday Meals

In this chapter, we will provide you Midday Meals that you can cook while camping.

5.1. Ranch Chicken Roll Ups

(Serves 2-4, Cook Time 10-20 Minutes, Difficulty: Normal)

Ingredients:

- 2 chicken breasts, cooked and shredded
- 12 oz cream cheese, softened
- 1 1/2 c cheddar cheese, shredded
- 1 c Monterey jack cheese, shredded
- 1 can crescent rolls
- Salt
- Pepper

Instructions:

1. Open a can of crescent rolls and separate triangles.

2. Add mixture to the large end of each crescent triangle and roll up, making sure triangles overlap.

3. Place aluminum foil over medium heat for 7 minutes or until crescent rolls are cooked through.

5.2. Cheesy Macaroni

(Serves 2, Cook Time 20 Minutes, Difficulty: Normal)

Ingredients:

- 1 tbsp butter
- 1/2 small onion, chopped
- 1 tbsp all-purpose flour
- 3/4 c milk
- 1 c cheddar cheese, grated
- 2 c elbow macaroni, cooked
- Salt and
- pepper

Instructions:

1. In a skillet, sauté onion in butter over medium for 5 min or until onion is tender.

2. Stir in flour and milk; continue stirring until thickened.

3. Add cheese and stir until melted. Add cooked macaroni and stir until heated—season to taste with salt and pepper before serving.

5.3. Dilled Bean and Tomato Salad

(Serves 4, Cook Time 15 Minutes, Difficulty: Normal)

Dressing:

- 1/4 c olive oil
- 2 tbsp lemon juice
- 1 tbsp balsamic vinegar Dill

Salad:

- 2 cans (19 oz) kidney beans, drained
- 2 cans (19 oz) chopped tomatoes, drained
- 2/3 c diced red onion
- Salt and ground black pepper

Instructions:

1. In a large bowl, toss kidney beans, tomatoes and onion.

2. Stir in olive oil mixture.

3. Season to taste with salt and pepper.

4. Cover and marinate at room temperature for 1 hour before serving.

5.4. Tomato Pasta Soup

(Serves 3-4, Cook Time 20 Minutes, Difficulty: Normal)

Ingredients:

- 1 pkg (2.5 oz) dried tomato soup
- 4 c water or milk
- 1/2 c dry elbow macaroni
- 4 wieners, sliced

Instructions:

1. In a medium saucepan, combine soup, water, or milk, and then bring to boil. Add macaroni and cook for 5 min.

2. Add wieners, cook for another 5 min.

3. Allow cooling for a few minutes before serving.

5.5. Bean Tacos

(Serves 4, Cook Time 20 Minutes, Difficulty: Normal)

Ingredients:

- 1 medium onion, chopped
- 2 garlic cloves, minced
- 2 tbsp butter
- 1 can (19oz) beans in tomato soup
- 1 tsp each cumin and chili powder
- 8 crisp taco shells or tortillas
- Chopped tomatoes and shredded lettuce (optional)

Instructions:

1. In a non-stick skillet, cook onion and garlic in butter until soft.

2. Stir in beans and seasonings, simmer over medium heat until hot.

3. Warm taco shells, spoon hot bean mixture into shells, top with cheese, tomato, and lettuce.

5.6. Huevos Rancheros

(Serves 2-4, Cook Time 20 Minutes, Difficulty: Normal)

Ingredients:

- 1 small onion, chopped
- 1/4 c chopped sweet green pepper
- 1 tbsp butter
- 2 c canned chopped tomatoes, drained
- 2 tsp chili powder
- 1 tsp garlic powder

- 4 eggs
- 4 flour tortillas salt and pepper

Instructions:

1. In a non-stick skillet, cook onion and green pepper in butter for 5 min.

2. Add tomatoes and seasonings and simmer for 10 min.

3. Break each egg into tomato mixture, cover and cook on medium heat until eggs are set about 5 min.

4. Warm tortillas; serve eggs with sauce over tortillas.

5.7. Grilled Ham and Cheese

(Serves 2, Cook Time 10 Minutes, Difficulty: Normal)

Ingredients:

- 4 slices of bread
- 2-4 slices ham
- 2 slices cheddar
- cheese

Instructions:

1. With a sandwich iron, place a slice of bread on each side of the iron.

2. Layer bread with 1-2 slices of ham and a slice of cheddar cheese.

3. Close sandwich iron and place over hot coals for 2 minutes or until bread is toasted on each side and cheese is melted.

4. Allow it to cool for a few minutes after removing it from the sandwich iron before eating.

5.8. Penne Pesto with Tuna

(Serves 4, Cook Time 20 Minutes, Difficulty: Normal)

Ingredients:

- 1 pkg (1 lb) penne pasta
- 2 pkgs (3 oz) tuna
- 2/3 c pesto sauce
- 1 large tomato, chopped
- 2 green onions, chopped

Instructions:

1. In a large pot of boiling water, cook penne according to package directions, about 8 min or until al dente; drain well.

2. Return to the pot, stir in tuna, pesto, tomato, and onions until combined.

5.9. Scrambled Eggs and Rice

(Serves 2, Cook Time 10 Minutes, Difficulty: Normal)

Ingredients:

- 1 tbsp butter
- 4 eggs
- 1 c cold cooked rice
- 1/4 c milk
- Salt and pepper to taste
- Hot sauce

Instructions:

1. In a nonstick skillet, melt butter over medium-low heat.

2. Add eggs, rice, milk, salt, pepper and hot sauce as desired.

3. Stir frequently, until eggs are cooked. Remove from heat and serve.

5.10. Salmon Sandwiches

(Serves 2, Cook Time 10 Minutes, Difficulty: Easy)

Ingredients:

- 1 pkg (3 oz) salmon
- 2 tbsp yogurt
- 1 tbsp vinegar
- 1 tbsp chopped onion
- 4 slices of bread
- Butter Chopped almonds
- Salt and pepper

Instructions:

1. In a bowl, flake salmon.

2. Add yogurt, vinegar, onion, almonds, salt and pepper to taste.

3. Toast bread over medium heat for approximately 2 minutes per side.

4. Spread butter on bread slices, top with salmon filling and close sandwich. Variations: In place of almonds, use walnuts, pecans or a mixture.

5.11. Quesadillas

(Serves 2, Cook Time 5-15 Minutes, Difficulty: Easy)

Ingredients:

- 4 large flour tortillas
- ½ c grated cheese
- 1 pkg (3 oz) tuna

- Chopped onions
- Salsa

Instructions:

1. Place the tortillas on a flat surface. Combine the cheese, tuna, onions, and enough salsa in a bowl to moisten the ingredients and keep them together. Divide the mixture over 2-tortillas on the surface, extending to the outside.

2. Cover with 2-left tortillas and press to close the corners. Over medium-high prepare, heat a large non-stick skillet.

3. Cook them one to brown all sides and melt the cheese, turn them over.

Chapter 6. BBQ & Campfire Recipes

In this chapter, we will provide you amazing and healthy BBQ recipes that you can cook while camping.

6.1. Classic Hamburgers

(Serves 4, Cook Time 10–12 minutes, Difficulty: Easy)

Ingredients:

- olive oil, for brushing
- 4 burger buns
- 2 tablespoons mustard
- shredded lettuce
- 2 tomatoes, sliced
- 2 dill pickles, sliced
- Burger mix
- 500 g (1 lb) rib-eye steak, minced
- 250 g (8 oz) skinless pork belly, minced

- 1 onion, finely chopped
- 1 teaspoon Worcestershire sauce
- 2 tablespoons capers, drained
- salt and pepper

Instructions:

1. Put the beef mince, pork mince, onion, Worcestershire sauce, capers, salt, and pepper in a bowl. Mix well, using your hands. Divide the mixture into 4 and shape it into even-sized burgers. Cover with cling film or put in a sealable plastic bag and chill in a cool box for 30 minutes.

2. Brush the burgers lightly with oil and cook on a grill rack over a hot barbecue or campfire for about 5–6 minutes on each side, or until lightly charred and cooked through.

3. Meanwhile, split the buns and toast into both sides on the rack. Spread the bottom halves with a little mustard, then fill with the shredded lettuce, burgers, tomato slices, and dill pickles. Top with the lids and serve.

6.2. Fast-Seared Steaks with French Beans

(Serves 4, Cook Time 5 minutes, Difficulty: Easy)

Ingredients:

- 400 g (13 oz) green beans, trimmed
- 1 teaspoon olive oil
- 4 thin steaks (such as feather steaks or frying steaks)
- 200 g (7 oz) rocket salad
- salt and pepper
- crusty bread, to serve
- Tomato dressing
- 2 tomatoes, diced

- 1 teaspoon olive oil
- 1 banana shallot, finely chopped
- 1 tablespoon wholegrain mustard
- 1 tablespoon red wine vinegar

Instructions:

1. Cook the green beans in a saucepan of lightly salted boiling water for about 2–3 minutes, or until tender but firm.

2. Meanwhile, to make the tomato dressing, mix all the ingredients in a bowl.

3. Drain the beans and return to the pan. Toss the tomato dressing through the beans, season well with salt and pepper, cover with a lid and keep warm.

4. Rub the oil over the steaks, then cook on a rack over a hot barbecue or campfire for 1 minute on each side, or until cooked to your liking.

5. Transfer to a plate, cover with foil and leave to rest for 1–2 minutes.

6. Divide the rocket salad onto plates. Spoon over the beans and dressing, then top with the steaks. Serve immediately with crusty bread.

6.3. Thai Chilly Beef Burgers

(Serves 4, Cook Time 10 Minutes, Difficulty: Easy)

Ingredients:

- olive oil, for brushing
- 1 baguette, cut into 4 and split lengthways
- shredded lettuce
- sweet chili sauce
- Burger mix
- 500 g (1 lb) minced beef
- 1 tablespoon Thai red curry paste

- 25 g (1 oz) fresh white breadcrumbs
- 2 tablespoons chopped fresh coriander
- 1 egg, lightly beaten
- 1 tablespoon light soy sauce
- Pepper

Instructions:

1. Put the minced beef in a bowl and stir in the red curry paste, breadcrumbs, coriander, egg, soy sauce, and pepper. Mix well using your hands. Divide the mixture into 8 and shape into mini burgers.

2. Brush the burgers lightly with oil and cook on a grill rack over a hot barbecue or campfire for about 4–5 minutes on each side, or until charred and cooked through.

3. Serve the burgers in the split bread with shredded lettuce and sweet chili sauce.

6.4. Sugar & Spice Glazed Beef

(Serves 4-5, Cook Time 30 Minutes, Difficulty: Normal)

Ingredients:

- 8 juniper berries
- 3 tablespoons black treacle
- 2 tablespoons light muscovado sugar
- 2 tablespoons whisky
- 2 tablespoons Worcestershire sauce
- 1 tablespoon grainy mustard
- ½ teaspoon finely ground black pepper
- 600 g (1¼ lb) piece of fillet steak
- salt

Instructions:

1. Crush the juniper berries using a pestle and mortar. Mix in a bowl with the treacle, sugar, whisky, Worcestershire sauce, mustard, and pepper.

2. Put the steak in a non-metallic dish and pour the marinade all over the surface. Cover loosely with clingfilm and leave to marinate in your cool box for about 1 hour.

3. Lift the meat from the dish, letting the excess marinade drip back into the dish, and season with a little salt. Transfer to a grill rack over a barbecue or campfire, cook for about 30 minutes and turn the meat frequently so it cooks reasonably evenly. Use a meat thermometer to test whether the beef is cooked to your liking. For rare, the temperature should register about 50°C (120°F). For well done, the meat should register 70–75°C (158–165°F) and will take longer to cook.

4. Pour the marinade juices into a small saucepan and heat through on the rack beside the meat. Transfer the meat to a board and carve into thick slices. Serve with the juices drizzled over.

6.5. Green Peppercorn Steaks

(Serves 4, Cook Time 10 Minutes, Difficulty: Easy)

Ingredients:

- 4 lean fillet steaks, about 75 g (3 oz) each
- 1 tablespoon green peppercorns in brine, drained
- 2 tablespoons light soy sauce
- 1 teaspoon balsamic vinegar
- 8 cherry tomatoes, halved

Instructions:

1. Heat a griddle pan on a grill rack over a hot barbecue or campfire until very hot.

2. Meanwhile, cook the steaks on the grill rack for 2–3 minutes on each side, or until cooked to your liking. Transfer to a plate, cover with foil and leave to rest while you make

the sauce.

3. Put the peppercorns, soy sauce, balsamic vinegar, and cherry tomatoes in the griddle pan. Leave the liquids to sizzle for a few minutes, or until the tomatoes are soft. Spoon the sauce over the steaks and serve.

6.7. Butterflied Leg of Lamb with Broad Bean & Dill Yogurt

(Serves 6, Cook Time 30-40 Minutes, Difficulty: Easy)

Ingredients:

Ingredients:

- 5 garlic cloves, crushed
- 4 handfuls of mint leaves, chopped
- 4 handfuls of parsley, chopped
- 3 tablespoons green peppercorns in brine, drained and crushed
- 2 tablespoons olive oil
- 1 butterflied leg of lamb, about 1.75 kg (3½ lb) in total
- Broad bean and dill yogurt
- 100 g (3½ oz) fresh baby broad beans
- 200 ml (7 Fl oz) Greek yogurt
- 4 tablespoons chopped dill
- salt

Instructions:

1. Mix the garlic, mint, parsley, peppercorns, and oil. Open out the lamb and spread the herb mixture all over the surface of the lamb. Place in a non-metallic dish and cover loosely with cling film. Leave to marinate for several hours or overnight in the cool box, allowing the meat to sit at room temperature for a couple of hours before cooking.

2. Make the yogurt, cook the beans in a saucepan of boiling water for 3–5 minutes until

tender. Drain and leave to cool. Pop the beans out of their skins and mix with the yogurt, dill, and a little salt. Transfer to a serving dish.

3. Transfer lamb to grill rack over the campfire and cook for 15–20 minutes on each side, until thoroughly browned the outside.

4. Place on a serving board or plate, cover with foil, and leave to rest for 15 minutes before slicing. Serve with the yogurt.

6.8. Aromatic Barbecued Lamb

(Serves 4, Cook Time 10-15 Minutes, Difficulty: Easy)

Ingredients:

- 4 lamb chump chops
- 2 cm (¾ inch) piece of fresh root ginger, peeled and grated
- 2 garlic cloves, crushed
- 1 red chilly, deseeded and thinly sliced
- 2 teaspoons dark muscovado sugar
- 3 tablespoons soy sauce
- 2 tablespoons dry sherry
- Fire-baked New Potatoes, to serve

Instructions:

1. Place the lamb chops in a shallow, non-metallic dish. Mix the ginger with the garlic, chili, sugar, soy sauce, and sherry and pour it over the lamb.

2. Turn the meat in the mixture, cover with clingfilm, and chill in a cool box for at least 2 hours or overnight.

3. Transfer the chops to a grill rack over a hot barbecue or campfire and cook for 3–8 minutes on each side, depending on whether you like the meat rare or well done. Use any excess marinade to baste the meat while it is cooking.

4. Serve with baked new potatoes.

6.10. Taverna-Style Lamb with Feta Salad

(Serves 4, Cook Time 15 Minutes, Difficulty: Easy)

Ingredients:

- 2 tablespoons chopped oregano
- 1 tablespoon chopped rosemary
- grated rind of 1 lemon
- 2 tablespoons olive oil
- salt and pepper
- 500 g (1 lb) leg or shoulder of lamb, diced
- crusty bread, to serve (optional)

Feta Salad:

- 200 g (7 oz) feta cheese, sliced
- 1 tablespoon chopped oregano
- 2 tablespoons chopped parsley
- grated rind and juice of 1 lemon
- ½ small red onion, finely sliced
- 3 tablespoons olive oil

Instructions:

1. Mix the herbs, lemon rind, oil, salt, and pepper in a non-metallic dish, add the lamb and mix to coat thoroughly. Thread the meat on to 4 metal skewers.

2. Arrange the sliced feta on a large serving dish and sprinkle over the herbs, lemon rind, and sliced onion. Drizzle over the lemon juice and oil and season with salt and pepper.

3. Cook lamb skewers on a grill rack over a hot barbecue or campfire for about 6–8

minutes, frequently turning until charred on the outside and almost cooked. Transfer to a plate, cover with foil, and leave to rest for 1–2 minutes.

4. Serve the lamb, with any pan juices poured over, with the salad and plenty of crusty bread, if liked.

6.11. Minted Lamb Kebabs

(Serves 4, Cook Time 7 Minutes, Difficulty: Easy)

Ingredients:

- 500 g (1 lb) minced lamb
- 1 small onion, finely chopped
- 1 garlic clove, crushed
- 1 tablespoon chopped rosemary
- 6 anchovies in oil, drained and chopped
- olive oil, for brushing
- salt and pepper
- Tomato and olive salad
- 6 tomatoes, cut into wedges
- 1 red onion, sliced
- 125 g (4 oz) pitted black olives
- a few torn basils leave
- 2 tablespoons olive oil
- a squeeze of lemon juice

Instructions:

1. Put the lamb, chopped onion, garlic, rosemary, anchovies, salt, and pepper in a bowl and mix using your hands. Divide the mixture into 12 and shape into even-sized, sausage-shaped patties. Cover with clingfilm and chill in the cool box for 30 minutes.

2. Thread the patties on to metal skewers, brush lightly with oil and cook on a grill rack over a hot barbecue or campfire for about 3–4 minutes on each side, or until cooked through.

3. Meanwhile, to make the salad, put the tomatoes, onion, olives, and basil in a bowl, season with salt and pepper, and mix. Drizzle with oil and squeeze a little lemon juice over. Serve the kebabs with the salad.

6.12. Barbecued Pork

(Serves 4, Cook Time 5-10 Minutes, Difficulty: Easy)

Ingredients:

- spare ribs
- 100 ml (3½ Fl oz) tomato ketchup
- 2 tablespoons clear honey
- 1 tablespoon dark soy sauce
- 1 tablespoon olive oil
- 1 tablespoon malt vinegar
- 2 teaspoons Dijon mustard
- 4 x 500 g (1 lb) packs pork spare ribs
- salt and pepper

Instructions:

1. Mix all ingredients except the pork in a bowl, then coat the ribs generously all over with the marinade.

2. Transfer to a grill rack over a barbecue or campfire and cook for about 20–30 minutes, occasionally basting with the marinade and frequently turning, until charred and tender.

6.13. Pork Escalopes with Lemon & Capers

(Serves 4, Cook Time 5 Minutes, Difficulty: Easy)

Ingredients:

- 1 tablespoon chopped flat leaf parsley
- 3 tablespoons chopped mint
- 4–6 tablespoons lemon juice
- 1 tablespoon capers, drained and chopped
- 6 tablespoons olive oil, plus extra for brushing
- 4 pork escalopes, about 125 g (4 oz) each, trimmed

Instructions:

1. Mix the herbs, lemon juice, capers, and oil in a bowl.

2. Brush the pork with oil and cook on a grill rack over a hot barbecue or campfire for about 2–3 minutes on each side, or until cooked through.

3. Drizzle the lemon and caper dressing over the pork and serve.

6.14. Sticky Gammon Steaks with Caramelized Onions

(Serves 4, Cook Time 25 Minutes, Difficulty: Easy)

Ingredients:

- a knob of butter
- 2 onions, sliced
- 2 teaspoons thyme leaves
- 4 tablespoons thick-cut marmalade
- 1 tablespoon wholegrain mustard
- 300 ml (½ pint) hot chicken stock
- 4 lean gammon steaks, about 100 g (3½ oz) each

- 1 tablespoon olive oil
- instant mashed potato, to serve (optional)

Instructions:

1. Melt the butter in a frying pan, add the onions and thyme leaves and cook over low heat, occasionally stirring, for about 15 minutes until softened and beginning to caramelize.

2. Stir in the marmalade, mustard, and stock, bring to the boil and then simmer gently for 2–3 minutes until beginning to thicken.

3. Brush the gammon steaks oil and cook on a grill rack over the campfire for about 15 minutes, until cooked through.

4. Add the steaks to the sauce and simmer for a further 3 minutes until the sauce is thick and sticky and the steaks are piping hot. Serve with instant mash, if liked.

6.15. Chorizo & Quail's Egg Pizzas
(Serves 2, Cook Time 20 Minutes, Difficulty: Easy)

Ingredients:

- 150 g (5 oz) strong white bread flour, plus extra for dusting
- ½ teaspoon fast-action dried yeast
- ½ teaspoon salt
- 1 tablespoon olive oil

Topping:

- 2 tablespoons olive oil, plus extra for drizzling
- 1 small garlic clove, crushed
- 75 g (3 oz) thinly sliced chorizo sausage
- 1 red chilly, deseeded and halved
- 100 g (3½ oz) Manchego cheese, grated

- 2 tablespoons pine nuts
- 6 quail's eggs
- salt and pepper
- rocket leaves, to scatter

Instructions:

1. To make the pizza base, mix the flour, yeast, salt and olive oil in a bowl and add 75 ml (3 Fl oz) hand-hot water. Mix with a round-bladed knife to

make a soft dough, adding a dash more water if the dough is dry.

2. Tip out on to a floured board and knead for about 10 minutes until the dough is smooth and elastic. (If you've no surface to work on, knead the dough in the bowl as best as you can.)

3. Return the dough to the bowl, cover with a clean tea towel or clingfilm and leave in a warm place (near the fire if already lit) until the dough has doubled in size. Heat a pizza spatula, pizza stone or sturdy baking sheet on a rack over a barbecue or campfire while assembling the pizza. Mix together the olive oil and garlic in a bowl.

4. Turn the dough out on to a floured surface and cut in half. Thinly roll out each piece to an oval shape measuring about 22 x 14 cm (8½ x 5½ inches) or to a size that allows you to fit them side by side on the baking sheet or pizza spatula or stone.

5. Transfer to the baking sheet or pizza stone and brush with the garlic oil. Scatter with the chorizo and add a chilly half to each. Sprinkle with the cheese and pine nuts and make 3 small indentations in each topping, then break the eggs into the wells and season with salt and pepper.

6. Make a dome of foil and position over the pizzas, tucking the ends under the base to secure. Cook for about 30 minutes, or until the bases are cooked and the eggs are softly set. Rotate the pizzas on the rack several times during cooking.

7. Serve scattered with rocket leaves and an extra drizzle of oil.

6.16. Seared Pork Chops with Chilli Corn

(Serves 4, Cook Time 10-20 Minutes, Difficulty: Easy)

Ingredients:

- 2 tablespoons olive oil
- 4 pork chops
- 200 g (7 oz) canned sweetcorn kernels
- 2 spring onions, thinly sliced
- 1 red chilly, chopped
- 5 tablespoons créme fraîche
- finely grated rind of 1 lime
- handful of coriander leaves, chopped
- salt and pepper

Instructions:

1. Brush the chops with half the oil and cook on a grill rack over a barbecue or campfire for about 5–10 minutes on each side (depending on thickness), or until golden and cooked through. Keep warm and allow to rest for 5 minutes.

2. Meanwhile, to make the chili corn, heat the remaining oil in a frying pan, add the sweetcorn and cook for 2 minutes until starting to brown, then stir in the spring onions and chili and cook for a further 1 minute.

3. Add the créme fraîche and lime rind and season to taste with salt and pepper. Scatter over the coriander and serve with the pork chops.

6.17. Spit-Roasted Pork with Apple Butter

(Serves 6, Cook Time 3–4 Hours, Difficulty: Hard)

Ingredients:

- 2 teaspoons fennel seeds, lightly crushed
- 2 teaspoons caraway seeds, lightly crushed
- 4 garlic cloves, crushed
- finely grated rind of 2 lemons
- 1 teaspoon freshly ground black pepper
- 2 kg (4 lb) shoulder of pork, skin and excess fat removed
- salt
- baps, baguettes or soft wraps, to serve
- Apple butter
- 500 g (1 lb) cooking apples, peeled, quartered and cored
- pinch of ground cloves
- 1 teaspoon caster sugar
- squeeze of lemon juice
- 4 tablespoons very soft slightly salted butter

Instructions:

1. Mix the fennel seeds, caraway seeds, garlic, lemon rind, pepper, and a little salt in a bowl. Make plenty of cuts over meat's surface with the tip of a knife, then push some of the spice mixtures into the cuts and spread the remainder all over the surface. Roll up and tie the pork at 3 cm (1¼ inch) intervals with kitchen string.

2. Skewer the pork onto a spit-roasting rod and set it up over a campfire or barbecue. Roast for about 3–4 hours, or until the pork is cooked through. Test the pork is cooked by pushing a meat thermometer into the thickest area of the meat. It should read about 75°C (165°F).

3. To make the butter, chop the apples into pieces and put them in a saucepan with a water dash. Cover with a lid and cook on the rack to one side of the pork until the apples are tender. You'll need to frequently add more water to stop the apples from burning on the base of the pan before they're soft. Once soft and mushy, remove from the heat, stir in the cloves, sugar, and lemon juice and leave to cool. Add the butter to the cooled apple mixture and beat well to mix.

4. Transfer the pork to a plate or board. Cover with foil and leave to rest in a warm place near the barbecue or fire for 15 minutes before removing the string. Carve into thick slices and serve in baps, baguettes, or soft wraps with the apple butter.

6.18. Chicken Satay Skewers

(Serves 4, Cook Time 20 Minutes, Difficulty: Easy)

Ingredients:

- 6 tablespoons dark soy sauce
- 2 tablespoons vegetable oil
- 1 teaspoon Chinese 5-spice powder
- 2–3 boneless, skinless chicken breasts, about 375 g (12 oz) in total, cut into
- long, thin strips
- cucumber, cut into strips, to serve
- Satay sauce
- 4 tablespoons peanut butter
- 1 tablespoon dark soy sauce
- ½ teaspoon ground coriander
- ½ teaspoon ground cumin
- pinch of paprika or chilly powder

Instructions:

1. Soak 8-wooden skewers in cold water for 30 minutes. Mix the soy sauce, oil, and 5-spice powder in a bowl. Add the chicken strips and toss together to coat in the marinade. Cover with clingfilm and leave to marinate in the cool box for 1-hour, stirring occasionally.

2. Thread the chicken, zigzag fashion, onto the soaked skewers. Transfer to a grill rack over a hot campfire and cook about 10 minutes, turning, until golden and cooked.

3. Meanwhile, put the sauce ingredients in a small saucepan with 8-tablespoons water and heat, stirring, until warm and well mixed.

4. Transfer to a small serving bowl. Serve the hot chicken skewers with the satay sauce and cucumber strips.

6.19. Lemon & Parsley Chicken Skewers

(Serves 2, Cook Time 10-15 Minutes, Difficulty: Easy)

Ingredients:

- 2 boneless, skinless chicken breasts, about 300 g (10 oz) in total, cut into
- chunks
- finely grated rind and juice of 1 lemon
- 2 tablespoons olive oil
- 3 tablespoons finely chopped parsley
- salt and pepper
- To serve
- rocket and tomato salad
- warm pitta breads
- 200 g (7 oz) tub tzatziki

Instructions:

1. Put the chicken in a bowl with the lemon rind and juice and the oil and toss well to coat. Stir in the parsley and season well with salt and pepper.

2. Thread the chicken on to 4 small metal skewers. Transfer to a grill rack over a hot barbecue or campfire and cook for about 10–15 minutes, turning once, until golden and cooked through.

3. Remove from the skewers and serve in warm pitta pieces of bread with a simple rocket and tomato salad and spoonful of tzatziki.

6.20. Tandoori Chicken Skewers with cucumber & cumin salad

(Serves 4, Cook Time 12 Minutes, Difficulty: Easy)

Ingredients:

- 175 g (6 oz) Greek yogurt, plus extra to serve
- 2 tablespoons tandoori paste
- 3–4 boneless, skinless chicken breasts, about 500 g (1 lb) in total, cut into
- thin strips
- 2 lemons, cut into wedges
- mini naan breads, to serve (optional)
- Cucumber salad
- 2 teaspoons cumin seeds
- 1 small cucumber
- 1 red onion, cut in half and finely sliced
- 3 tablespoons coriander leaves
- salt and pepper

Instructions:

1. Mix the yogurt and tandoori paste in a bowl, add the chicken and toss until the chicken is well coated. Cover with clingfilm and leave to marinate for 10 minutes.

2. Heat a frying pan over medium heat, add the cumin seeds, and dry-roast for 1–2 minutes, stirring frequently. Remove from the heat when the seeds become fragrant and begin to smoke.

3. Thread the chicken strips on to 8-small metal skewers. Transfer to a grill rack over a hot barbecue or campfire and cook for about 10 minutes, turning once, until cooked through.

4. Meanwhile, slice the cucumber into ribbons using a sharp vegetable peeler and arrange on plates. Scatter the onion and coriander over the cucumber, sprinkle over the toasted cumin seeds, and season lightly with salt and pepper. Place the chicken on top and serve with lemon wedges, extra yogurt, and warm naan pieces of bread, if liked.

6.21. Blackened Chicken Skewers

(Serves 4-6, Cook Time 20 Minutes, Difficulty: Normal)

Ingredients:

- 2 boneless, skinless chicken breasts, about 300 g (10 oz), cut into chunks
- 1 tablespoon Cajun seasoning mix
- 2 tablespoons lemon juice
- 1 teaspoon olive oil

To serve:

- Garlic Bread
- green salad

Instructions:

1. Soak 8-wooden skewers in cold water for 30 minutes. Put the chicken in a bowl, add the seasoning mix, lemon juice, and olive oil and toss together well. Cover with clingfilm and leave to marinate for 15 minutes.

2 Thread the chicken onto the soaked skewers. Transfer to a grill rack over a hot barbecue or campfire and cook for about 10–15 minutes, turning once, until cooked through.

3. Serve with garlic bread and a green salad.

6.22. Chicken Burgers with Tomato Salsa

(Serves 4, Cook Time 6-8 Minutes, Difficulty: Easy)

Ingredients:

- 1 garlic clove, crushed
- 3 spring onions, finely sliced
- 1 tablespoon ready-made pesto
- 2 tablespoons chopped fresh mixed herbs (such as parsley, tarragon and thyme)
- 375 g (12 oz) minced chicken
- 2 sun-dried tomatoes, finely chopped
- 1 teaspoon olive oil
- Tomato salsa
- 250 g (8 oz) cherry tomatoes, quartered
- 1 red chilly, cored, deseeded and finely chopped
- 1 tablespoon chopped fresh coriander
- grated rind and juice of 1 lime

Instructions:

1. Mix all the burger ingredients except the oil in a bowl. Divide the mixture into 4 and shape it into even-sized flattened rounds. Cover with clingfilm and chill in a cool box for 30 minutes.

2. Meanwhile, combine all the tomato salsa ingredients in a bowl. Brush the burgers lightly with the oil and cook on a grill rack over a hot barbecue or campfire for about 3–4 minutes on each side, or until cooked through. Serve immediately with the salsa.

6.23. Chicken & Mozzarella Skewers

(Serves 4, Cook Time 20 Minutes, Difficulty: Easy

Ingredients:

- 8 small boneless, skinless chicken thigh fillets
- 2 bocconcini balls (baby mozzarellas), quartered
- 8 large basil leaves
- 8 large slices of prosciutto
- 2 small lemons, halved
- salt and pepper

Instructions:

1. Lay the chicken thighs flat on a plate, boned side up, and season with a little salt and pepper. Place a quarter of bocconcini and a basil leaf in each center, then roll up to enclose the filling. Wrap each thigh in a slice of prosciutto and thread on to 8 metal skewers, using 2-skewers for 2-parcels (this makes them easier to turn).

2. Transfer the skewers to a grill rack over a hot barbecue or campfire and cook for about 8 minutes on each side, or until cooked through and the mozzarella starts to ooze. Transfer to a plate, cover with foil, and leave to rest for 5 minutes.

3. Meanwhile, cook the lemon halves, cut side down, for 5 minutes until charred and tender. Serve the skewers drizzled with lemon juice.

6.24. Herb-Marinated Spatchcock Chicken

(Serves 4, Cook Time 40 Minutes, Difficulty: Easy)

Ingredients:

- 1 teaspoon cumin seeds, lightly crushed
- 2 garlic cloves, crushed
- 2 handfuls of parsley, chopped

- 2 handfuls of coriander leaves, chopped
- ¼ teaspoon dried chilly flakes
- 1 tablespoon vegetable oil
- 1 tablespoon clear honey
- finely grated rind of 1 lemon
- 2 teaspoons lemon juice
- 1 whole chicken, about 1.5 kg (3 lb)
- salt

To serve:
- leafy salad
- new potatoes

Instructions:

1. Mix the cumin seeds, garlic, parsley, coriander, chili flakes, oil, honey and lemon rind, and juice in a bowl.

2. To spatchcock the chicken, place the chicken on a board, breast side down. Using sturdy kitchen scissors, cut along one side of the backbone, then the other to obliterate the backbone. Turn the bird over, breast side up, and flatten out the legs, so they face inwards. Use the heel of your hand to push the breastbone firmly down and flatten out the chicken thoroughly.

3. Push a wooden skewer diagonally through the bird, so the skewer goes through one leg then out through the wing on the other side. Push another skewer through in the opposite direction. Spread the herb mixture over the chicken on both sides and place on a plate. Cover loosely with clingfilm and leave to marinate in a cool box for several hours.

4. Season the chicken lightly with salt on both sides. Transfer to a grill rack over a barbecue or campfire and cook for about 20 minutes on each side or until the juices run clear when the chicken's thickest part is pierced with a sharp knife. If the chicken skin starts to burn before the chicken is cooked through, wrap it in foil and move it to one side of the rack to cook more gently.

5. Transfer the chicken to a large board or plate, cover with foil, and leave to rest for 5 minutes; chop the chicken into pieces and serve with salad and new potatoes.

6.25. Spit-Roasted Chicken with Saffron Mayonnaise

(Serves 4, Cook Time 1-2 Hours, Difficulty: Easy)

Ingredients:

- 2 teaspoons ground paprika
- 1 teaspoon fennel seeds, lightly crushed
- ½ teaspoon celery seeds
- 2 garlic cloves, finely chopped
- ½ teaspoon freshly ground black pepper
- 1 whole chicken, about 1.5 kg (3 lb)
- small handful of bay leaves, thyme and parsley
- salt
- Saffron mayonnaise
- good pinch of saffron strands
- 100 ml (3 Fl oz) crème fraîche
- 100 g (3 oz) mayonnaise

Instructions:

1. Put the paprika, fennel seeds, celery seeds, garlic, and pepper in a large plastic freezer bag and shake the bag to mix the ingredients.

2. Add the chicken to the bag. Balloon out the bag, twisting the open end to secure, and turn the chicken in the spice mixture until coated. Tie loosely and leave to marinate in a cool box for several hours or overnight.

3. Push the herbs into the chicken cavity. Skewer the chicken onto a spit roasting rod and set it up over a campfire or barbecue. Sprinkle with a little salt and roast for about 1½–2 hours, or until the chicken is cooked through.

4. The juices should run clear when the thickest part of the thigh is pierced with

the tip of a sharp knife.

5. To make the mayonnaise, crumble the saffron into a mug and add one teaspoon of boiling water. Leave to stand for 5 minutes. Beat the crème fraîche and mayonnaise together in a bowl with a little salt and pepper. Stir in the saffron and liquid.

6. Transfer the chicken to a plate or board and cover it with foil. Leave to rest in a warm place near the barbecue or fire for 15 minutes before carving.

7. Serve with the mayonnaise.

6.26. Chicken Fajitas

(Serves 4, Cook Time 5 Minutes, Difficulty: Easy)

Ingredients:

- ½ teaspoon ground coriander
- ½ teaspoon ground cumin
- ½ teaspoon ground paprika
- 1 garlic clove, crushed
- 3 tablespoons chopped fresh coriander
- 2–3 boneless, skinless chicken breasts, about 375 g (12 oz) in total, cut into
- bite-sized strips
- 1 tablespoon olive oil

- 4 soft flour tortillas
- soured cream, to serve (optional)
- Salsa
- 3 large ripe tomatoes, finely chopped
- 3 tablespoons chopped fresh coriander
- ⅛ cucumber, finely chopped
- 1 tablespoon olive oil
- Guacamole
- 1 large avocado, peeled, stone removed and roughly chopped
- grated rind and juice of ½ lime
- 2 teaspoons sweet chilly sauce (optional)

Ingredients:

1. Put all the ground spices, garlic, and chopped coriander in a bowl. Toss the chicken in the oil, then add to the spices and toss to coat lightly in the spice mixture. Cover with clingfilm and leave to marinate while you make the salsa.

2. To make the salsa, mix the tomatoes, coriander, and cucumber in a bowl and drizzle over the oil.

3. Make the guacamole, in a separate bowl, mash together the avocado, lime rind and juice, and sweet chili sauce, if using, until soft and rough-textured. Heat a griddle pan or frying pan on a grill rack over a barbecue or campfire until hot, add the chicken and cook for about 5 minutes, occasionally turning, until golden and cooked through.

4. Fill the tortillas with the hot chicken strips, guacamole, and salsa. Fold into quarters and serve with a little soured cream, if liked.

6.27. Thai Barbecued Chicken

(Serves 4, Cook Time 40 Minutes, Difficulty: Easy)

Ingredients:

- 1 whole chicken, about 1.5 kg (3 lb), spatchcocked
- 5 cm (2 inch) piece of fresh galangal or root ginger, peeled and finely
- chopped
- 4 garlic cloves, crushed
- 1 large red chilly, finely chopped
- 4 shallots, finely chopped
- 2 tablespoons finely chopped fresh coriander
- 150 ml (¼ pint) canned coconut milk
- salt and pepper
- To serve
- sweet chilly sauce
- lime wedges
- boiled rice

Ingredients:

1. Rub the chicken all over with salt and pepper and place in a shallow dish. Mix the remaining ingredients in a jug until well blended, then pour over the chicken. Cover loosely with clingfilm and leave to marinate in a cool box for several hours or overnight.

2. Transfer the chicken from the marinade to a grill rack over a hot barbecue or campfire and cook for about 20 minutes on each side, turning and frequently basting with the remaining marinade until the juices run clear when the thickest part of the chicken is pierced with a sharp knife.

3. If the chicken skin starts to burn before the chicken is cooked through, wrap it in foil and move to one side of the rack so it can cook more gently. Transfer the chicken to a large board or plate, cover with foil and leave 3to rest for 5 minutes, then chop it into small pieces. Serve with sweet chili sauce, lime wedges, and boiled rice.

6.28. Prawn & Bacon Skewers
(Serves 4, Cook Time 4-6 Minutes, Difficulty: Easy)

Ingredients:

- 4 streaky bacon rashers, rind removed
- 12 raw peeled large prawns, deveined but tails intact
- 12 cherry tomatoes
- 12 basil leaves
- olive oil, for brushing
- salt and pepper
- lemon wedges, to serve

Ingredients:

1. Soak 12 wooden skewers in cold water for 30 minutes. Cut each bacon rasher into 3-pieces crossways, then run the back of a knife along each piece's length to stretch them out thinly.

2. Wrap each prawn carefully with bacon and thread onto a soaked skewer with a tomato and basil leaf. Season each skewer with a little salt and pepper.

3. Brush the skewers with a little oil and cook on a grill rack over a hot barbecue or campfire for 2–3 minutes on each side, or until the prawns turn pink and are cooked through. Serve hot with the lemon wedges for squeezing over.

6.29. Scallop & Chorizo Skewers

(Serves 4, Cook Time 10 Minutes, Difficulty: Easy)

Ingredients:

- 12 scallops, white meat only
- 12 large sage leaves
- 150 g (5 oz) chorizo sausage, cut into 12 x 1 cm (½ inch) pieces
- 2 tablespoons olive oil
- 1 tablespoon lemon juice
- 1 garlic clove, crushed
- salt and pepper
- lemon wedges, to serve

Instructions:

1. Soak 12 small wooden skewers in cold water for 30 minutes. Wrap each scallop with a sage leaf, thread it onto the soaked skewers with the chorizo pieces, and then transfer to a dish.

2. Mix the oil, lemon juice, garlic, salt, and pepper in a bowl, and then drizzle over the skewers. Cover with clingfilm and leave to marinate in a cool box for 1 hour.

3. Cook the skewers on a grill rack over a hot barbecue or campfire for 2–3 minutes on each side, or until the scallops are cooked through. Serve hot with lemon wedges for squeezing over.

6.30. Quick Tuna Steaks with green salsa

(Serves 4, Cook Time 10-15 Minutes, Difficulty: Easy)

Ingredients:

- 2 tablespoons olive oil
- grated rind of 1 lemon

- 2 teaspoons chopped parsley
- ½ teaspoon crushed coriander seeds
- 4 tuna steaks, about 150 g (5 oz) each
- salt and pepper
- crusty bread, to serve
- Salsa
- 2 tablespoons capers, drained and chopped
- 2 tablespoons chopped cornichons
- 1 tablespoon finely chopped parsley
- 2 teaspoons chopped chives
- 2 teaspoons finely chopped chervil
- 30 g (1 oz) pitted green olives, chopped
- 1 shallot, finely chopped (optional)
- 2 tablespoons lemon juice
- 2 tablespoons olive oil

Instructions:

1. Mix the oil, lemon rind, parsley, coriander seeds, and plenty of pepper in a bowl. Rub the tuna steaks with the mixture and set aside.

2. To make the salsa, mix the ingredients in a bowl, season to taste with salt and pepper, and set aside.

3. Cook the tuna on a grill rack over a hot barbecue or campfire for 1–2 minutes on each side, or until well charred on the outside but still pink in the middle. Alternatively, cook for a little less time, or for longer, until cooked to your liking.

4. Transfer the tuna to a plate, cover with foil, and leave to rest for a few minutes. Serve with the salsa and plenty of fresh crusty bread.

6.31. Blackened Tuna with Mango Salsa

(Serves 4, Cook Time 10 Minutes, Difficulty: Easy)

Ingredients:

- 4 tuna steaks, about 250 g (8 oz) each
- 1 tablespoon olive oil
- 2 tablespoons freshly crushed black peppercorns
- 1 teaspoon salt lime wedges, to serve
- Mango salsa
- 1 large mango, about 500 g (1 lb), peeled, stoned and diced
- ½ red onion, finely chopped
- 1 large red chilly, deseeded and finely chopped
- 1 tablespoon lime juice
- 2 tablespoons chopped fresh coriander
- salt and pepper

Instructions:

1. To make the mango salsa, mix all the ingredients in a bowl and season to taste with salt and pepper. Leave to stand to allow the flavors to develop.

2. Brush the tuna steaks with a little oil and season with the peppercorns and salt. Cook on a grill rack over a hot barbecue or campfire for about 1–2 minutes on each side, or until well seared on the outside but still pink in the middle. Alternatively, cook for a little less time, or for longer, until cooked to your liking.

3. Transfer the tuna to a plate, cover with foil and leave to rest for a few minutes, then serve with the salsa and lime wedges for squeezing over.

6.32. Swordfish Steaks with Basil & Pine Nut Oil

(Serves 4, Cook Time 10 Minutes, Difficulty: Easy)

Ingredients:

- 1 teaspoon olive oil
- 4 swordfish steaks, about 150 g (5 oz) each
- 250 g (8 oz) herby baby leaf salad
- 75 g (3 oz) ready-to-eat, slow-roasted tomatoes, roughly chopped
- salt and pepper
- Basil and pine nut oil
- 1 small bunch of basil, leaves stripped
- 5 teaspoons olive oil
- 1 tablespoon toasted pine nuts
- 1 tablespoon lemon juice

Instructions:

1. Brush the oil over the swordfish steaks and season well with salt and pepper. Cook on a grill rack over a barbecue or campfire for about 5–7 minutes, turning once until nicely charred on the outside but still slightly pink in the middle.

2. Meanwhile, to make the basil oil, crush all the ingredients in a pestle and mortar, then season with salt and pepper. Alternatively, finely chop the basil and pine nuts and mix them with the oil and lemon juice.

3. Pile the baby leaf salad onto plates and scatter with the slow-roasted tomatoes. Transfer the swordfish to the plates and serve with a little basil oil drizzled over.

6.33. Olive & Citrus Salmon

(Serves 4, Cook Time 8-10 Minutes, Difficulty: Easy)

Ingredients:

- 4 salmon fillets, about 200 g (7 oz) each
- 12 large black olives, pitted and halved
- 12 cherry tomatoes, halved
- 4 tablespoons olive oil
- 2 lemon wedges, thinly sliced
- 2 teaspoons clear honey
- salt and pepper
- chopped parsley, to garnish
- Tabbouleh, to serve

Instructions:

1. Remove any stray bones from the salmon fillets. Place the fish on 4-large pieces of heavy-duty foil and top each with a quarter of the olives, tomatoes, oil, lemon, and honey. Season with salt and pepper, then bring the foil up around the fish and seal well.

2. Cook the parcels on a grill rack over a hot barbecue or campfire for about 8–10 minutes, or until the fish is cooked through, then transfer to a plate and leave to rest for a few minutes.

3. Carefully open the parcels, sprinkle with chopped parsley, and serve with tabbouleh.

6.34. Stuffed Salmon Fillets with Pancetta & Tomatoes

(Serves 5-6, Cook Time 40 Minutes, Difficulty: Easy)

Ingredients:

- 3 shallots, thinly sliced
- 3 garlic cloves, finely chopped

- 100 g (3½ oz) sun-dried tomatoes in oil, drained and chopped
- 3 tablespoons chopped tarragon
- 2 x 500 g (1 lb) skinless salmon fillets
- 6 thin streaky bacon or pancetta rashers
- salt and pepper

Instructions:

1. Mix the shallots, garlic, sun-dried tomatoes, tarragon, and a little salt and pepper in a bowl.

2. Remove any stray bones from the salmon fillets. Place one fillet, skinned side up, on a board and spread the shallot mixture on top. Cover with the remaining salmon fillet, skinned side down. Space the bacon or pancetta rashers across the salmon, tucking any long ends underneath. Tie kitchen string around the salmon to hold the fillets together and secure the bacon rashers in place.

3. Brush a grill rack with oil and place over a barbecue or campfire fire.

4. Cook the salmon for 20–30 minutes on each side, or until cooked through, turning the fish over several times to check that it's not burning on the underside.

5. Transfer to a board or plate and cut away the string. Serve in chunky slices.

6.35. Mackerel with Citrus Fennel Salad

(Serves 4, Cook Time 8-10 Minutes, Difficulty: Easy)

Ingredients:

- 4 mackerel, about 400 g (13 oz) each
- olive oil, for brushing
- 3 lemons, thinly sliced
- Fennel salad
- 1 fennel bulb, trimmed and thinly sliced, fronds reserved

- 1 small garlic clove, crushed
- 2 tablespoons capers, drained
- 2 tablespoons olive oil
- 1 tablespoon chopped parsley
- 2 tablespoons lemon juice
- salt and pepper

Instructions:

1. Slash each mackerel 3–4 times on each side with a sharp knife. Brush with a little oil and season inside and out with salt and pepper. Using kitchen string, tie 3-lemon slices on each side of the fish.

2. Brush with a little more oil and cook on a grill rack over a hot barbecue or campfire for 4–5 minutes on each side, or until lightly charred and cooked through. Cover with foil and leave to rest for 5 minutes.

3. Toss together the fennel slices and fronds, garlic, capers, oil, parsley, and lemon juice in a bowl, then season to taste with salt and pepper. Serve the mackerel with the fennel salad.

6.36. Mackerel Fillets with Pickled Beetroot

(Serves 2, Cook Time 15 Minutes, Difficulty: Easy)

Ingredients:

- 175 g (6 oz) fresh beetroot, grated
- 3 tablespoons finely chopped dill
- 2 shallots, finely chopped
- 2 teaspoons white wine vinegar
- 1 teaspoon caster sugar
- 4 small mackerel fillets

- salt and pepper
- a knob of butter, cubed
- Herb yogurt
- 4 tablespoons Greek yogurt
- 2 tablespoons finely chopped parsley
- squeeze of lemon juice

Instructions:

1. Mix the beetroot, dill, shallots, vinegar, sugar, and a little salt and pepper in a bowl. Put 2-mackerel fillets on a board, skin side down, and spread the beetroot mixture on top. Place the remaining fillets, skin side up, on top to sandwich the filling.

2. Transfer the stuffed fillets to 2 large squares of heavy-duty foil and dot with the butter, then bring the foil up around the fish and seal well. Tuck between hot coals or logs to cook for about 20–30 minutes, or until the mackerel is cooked through. Rotate the parcels once or twice during cooking.

3. Meanwhile, beat the yogurt, parsley, lemon juice, and a little salt and pepper in a bowl. Serve with the fish.

6.37. Chargrilled Sardines with mango & lime salsa

(Serves 4, Cook Time 10-15 Minutes, Difficulty: Easy)

Ingredients:

- 1 teaspoon peeled and finely grated fresh root ginger
- finely grated rind and juice of 1 lime
- 1 small bunch of coriander, roughly chopped
- 1 tablespoon vegetable oil
- ½ large red chilly, deseeded and chopped
- 12–16 fresh sardines, scaled, gutted and cleaned

- Mango and lime salsa
- 1 firm, ripe mango, peeled, stoned and diced
- 4 tomatoes, deseeded and diced
- 1 spring onion, finely chopped
- 2 tablespoons lime juice
- ½ large red chilly, deseeded and chopped

Instructions:

1. Crush together the ginger, lime rind, juice, coriander, oil, and chili in a pestle and mortar to make a rough paste.

2. Score small slits into the sardine flesh, then rub the paste all over, massaging it into the slits.

3. Cook the sardines on a grill rack over a hot barbecue or campfire for about 3–4 minutes on each side, or until cooked through and slightly blackened.

4. Meanwhile, to make the salsa, mix all the ingredients in a small bowl. Serve with the sardines.

6.38. Salt & Pepper Tiger Prawns with Baby Corn & Mango Salsa
(Serves 4, Cook Time 15 Minutes, Difficulty: Easy)

Ingredients:

- 1 teaspoon coarse sea salt
- 1 teaspoon Chinese 5-spice powder
- 1 teaspoon cracked black pepper
- ½ teaspoon Szechuan peppercorns, crushed
- pinch of cayenne pepper
- 500 g (1 lb) raw tiger prawns, with shells on, rinsed
- 8 soft flour tortillas, to serve

- Baby corn and mango salsa
- 200 g (7 oz) baby corn, sliced into small rounds
- 2 spring onions, trimmed and finely chopped
- 1 chilly, deseeded and finely chopped
- 1 small mango, peeled, stoned and diced
- 2 tablespoons sweet soy sauce (ketjap manis)

Instructions:

1. Mix the sea salt, Chinese 5-spice powder, black, Szechuan, and cayenne peppers in a large bowl, then tip in the prawns and toss until well coated in the spices.

2. Heat a griddle pan over a barbecue or campfire until very hot, arrange the prawns over the pan and cook for about 4–5 minutes, or until the prawns turn pink and are cooked through but still juicy.

3. Meanwhile, to make the baby corn and mango salsa, mix the baby corn, spring onions, red chili, and diced mango in a bowl, then stir in the sweet soy sauce.

4. Serve the prawns with the tortillas and the baby corn and mango salsa (and a large bowl for the shells).

6.39. Prawns with Piri

(Serves 6, Cook Time 10 Minutes, Difficulty: Easy)

Ingredients:

- 3 tablespoons olive oil
- grated rind and juice of 1 lemon
- 2 teaspoons piri piri seasoning
- 2 teaspoons tomato purée
- 2 garlic cloves, finely chopped
- 400 g (13 oz) raw tiger prawns, shells on and heads removed, rinsed

- salt and pepper
- chopped parsley, to garnish
- lemon wedges, to serve

Instructions:

1. Mix the oil, lemon rind and juice,b Piri seasoning, tomato purée, garlic, salt, and pepper in a bowl. Add the prawns and toss until evenly coated. Cover with clingfilm and leave to marinate in a cool box for at least 2 hours.

2. Thread the prawns on 12 metal skewers through the thickest part of the body and tail. Transfer to a grill rack over a hot barbecue or campfire and cook for about 5–6 minutes, turning once, until the prawns turn pink and are cooked through.

3. Sprinkle the prawns with chopped parsley and serve with lemon wedges for squeezing over

6.40. Potato & Cheese Burgers

(Serves 6, Cook Time 30 Minutes, Difficulty: Easy)

Ingredients:

- 750 g (1½ lb) red or waxy potatoes, unpeeled
- 200 g (7 oz) mild Cheddar cheese, grated
- 1 red onion, finely chopped
- 2 tablespoons butter
- salt and pepper
- To serve (optional)
- smoked trout fillets
- cucumber slices

Instructions:

1. Cook the potatoes in a large saucepan of boiling water for about 20 minutes, or until just cooked but firm. Drain and leave to cool.

2. Peel the potatoes and grate them into a bowl. Stir in the grated cheese and chopped onion and season with salt and pepper. Divide the mixture into 6 and shape into rounds using wet hands, then press down with two fingers to form into burgers. Neaten up the edges.

3. Melt half the butter in a griddle pan or frying pan over a barbecue or campfire, add half the burgers, and cook for about 5 minutes, turning once, until golden brown and heated through. Transfer to a plate, then repeat with the remaining butter and burgers.

4. Serve the burgers warm or cold with lightly smoked trout fillets and cucumber slices, if liked.

6.41. Cheddar Burgers with Cucumber Salsa

(Serves 4, Cook Time 20 Minutes, Difficulty: Easy)

Ingredients:

- 200 g (7 oz can) butter beans, drained
- 1 onion, finely chopped
- 1 carrot, grated
- 100 g (3½ oz) mature Cheddar cheese, grated
- 100 g (3½ oz) fresh breadcrumbs
- 1 egg
- 1 teaspoon cumin seeds
- vegetable oil, for frying
- 4 round French rolls
- salt and pepper

- Cucumber salsa
- ½ small cucumber
- 2 tablespoons chopped fresh coriander
- 2 spring onions, finely chopped
- 1 tablespoon lemon or lime juice
- 1 teaspoon caster sugar

Instructions:

1. Place the butter beans in a bowl and lightly mash them with a fork. Add the onion, carrot, cheese, breadcrumbs, egg, cumin seeds, salt, and pepper and mix until evenly combined.

2. Divide the mixture into 4-and shape them into small flat cakes. Heat a little oil in a griddle pan or frying pan over a barbecue or campfire and cook the burgers for about 8 minutes, turning once, until crisp, golden, and heated through.

3. Meanwhile, halve the cucumber for the salsa, scoop out the seeds, and finely chop. Toss in a bowl with the coriander, spring onions, lemon or lime juice, sugar, and a little salt and pepper.

4. Split the rolls and fill them with the burgers and salsa.

6.42. Mushroom, Couscous & Herb Sausages
(Serves 6, Cook Time 30 Minutes, Difficulty: Easy)

Ingredients:

- 75 g (3 oz) couscous
- 3 tablespoons olive oil, plus extra for brushing
- 1 onion, finely chopped
- 250 g (8 oz) chestnut mushrooms, finely chopped
- 1 red chilly, deseeded and finely sliced

- 3 garlic cloves, finely chopped
- small handful of mixed herbs (such as thyme, rosemary and parsley), finely chopped
- 200 g (7 oz) whole cooked chestnuts, finely chopped
- 75 g (3 oz) fresh breadcrumbs
- 1 egg yolk
- flour, for dusting
- salt and pepper

Instructions:

1. Put the couscous in a heatproof bowl and add 75 ml (3 Fl oz) boiling water. Cover with clingfilm and leave to stand for 5 minutes, then fluff up with a fork.

2. Meanwhile, heat the olive oil in a frying pan, add the onion, mushrooms, and chili and fry over high heat for about 5 minutes until the mushrooms are golden and the moisture has evaporated.

3. Turn into a bowl, add the remaining ingredients and couscous and mix well. Divide the mixture into 12 and shape into sausage shapes using lightly floured hands. Cover with clingfilm and chill in a cool box for 30 minutes.

4. Brush the sausages with a little oil and cook on a grill rack over a barbecue or campfire for about 10 minutes, turning frequently, until golden and piping hot in the middle.

6.43. Tomato, Pesto & Olive Pizzas

(Serves 6, Cook Time 20-25 Minutes, Difficulty: Easy)

Ingredients:

- 250 g (8 oz) strong white bread flour, plus extra for dusting
- ½ teaspoon salt
- 1 teaspoon fast-action dried yeast

- 1 tablespoon olive oil, plus extra for brushing and drizzling

Topping

- 2 tablespoons ready-made pesto
- 200 g (7 oz) cherry tomatoes, halved
- 150 g (5 oz) mozzarella cheese, sliced
- 50 g (2 oz) pitted black olives, halved
- handful of basil leaves
- salt and pepper

Ingredients:

1. To make the pizza base, mix the flour, salt, and yeast in a bowl. Make a well in the center, add 125 ml (4 Fl oz) hand-hot water and the oil and mix with a round-bladed knife until the mixture comes together in a ball. Tip out onto a floured board and knead for about 10 minutes until the dough is smooth and elastic. (If you've no surface to work on, work the dough in the bowl as best as you can.) Return the dough to the bowl, cover with a clean tea towel or clingfilm and leave in a warm place (near the fire if already lit) until doubled in size.

2. Punch the dough to deflate it, then cut it in half. Roll out one piece on a floured board to a roundabout 23 cm (9 inches) in diameter. Lightly brush a heavy-based frying pan with oil and press the dough into the base.

3. Spread half the pesto over the dough and top with half the tomatoes, mozzarella and olives, salt and pepper, and a drizzle more oil.

4. Place the pan on a grill rack over a moderately hot barbecue or campfire, make a dome of foil, and position over the pizza, tucking the ends under the base to secure. Cook for 10–12 minutes until the base is crisp underneath and the cheese melted.

5. Carefully slide the pizza out onto a board, sprinkle with half the basil leaves, and serve hot. Repeat with the remaining ingredients to make the second pizza.

6.44. Double Cheese Margherita Pizza

(Serves 4, Cook Time 30 Minutes, Difficulty: Easy)

Ingredients:

- 275 g (9 oz) strong white bread flour, plus extra for dusting
- 1 teaspoon fast-action dried yeast
- 1 teaspoon salt
- 2 tablespoons olive oil

Topping:

- 225 g (7½ oz) can chop tomatoes
- 2 tablespoons sun-dried tomato paste
- 1 teaspoon caster sugar
- 1 small garlic clove, crushed
- 250 g (8 oz) mozzarella cheese, thinly sliced
- 75 g (3 oz) Parmesan cheese, grated
- handful of pitted black olives
- salt and pepper

Ingredients:

1. To make the pizza base, mix the flour, yeast, salt, and olive oil in a bowl and add 175 ml (6 Fl oz) hand-hot water. Mix with a round-bladed knife to make a soft dough, adding a dash more water if the dough feels dry. Tip out onto a floured board and knead for about 10 minutes until the dough is smooth and elastic. (If you've no surface to work on, work the dough in the bowl as best as you can.) Return the dough to the bowl, cover with a clean tea towel or clingfilm and leave in a warm place (near the fire if already lit) until doubled in size.

2. Heat a pizza spatula, pizza stone, or sturdy baking sheet on a rack over the fire while assembling the pizza. Turn the dough out onto a floured board and roll out to a roundabout 30 cm (12 inches) in diameter. Transfer to the baking sheet, stone, or spatula.

3. Mix the tomatoes, tomato paste, sugar, garlic, and a little salt and pepper and spread over the base to about 1 cm (½ inch) from the edges. Arrange the mozzarella slices on top and scatter with the Parmesan.

4. Sprinkle with the olives and season with salt and pepper. Make a dome of foil and position it over the pizza, tucking the ends under the base to secure.

5. Cook for about 30 minutes, or until the base is cooked and the cheese is melting.

6.45. Indian Spiced Sweet Potatoes

(Serves 4, Cook Time 1-2 Hours, Difficulty: Easy)

Ingredients

- 800–900 g (1 lb 10 oz–1 lb 14 oz) sweet potatoes, scrubbed
- 25 g (1 oz) firm creamed coconut, grated
- 8 cardamom pods, crushed to release the seeds
- 2 garlic cloves, finely chopped
- 1 small hot chilly, deseeded and finely chopped
- 3 tablespoons chopped fresh coriander
- 2 tablespoons vegetable oil
- Salt

Instructions:

1. Cut the potatoes across into 1 cm (½ inch) thick slices and place in the centers of 4 large squares of heavy-duty foil.

2. Mix the coconut, cardamom, garlic, chili, and 2-tablespoons of the coriander in a bowl. Spoon the mixture over the potatoes and drizzle with the oil. Bring the foil up around the filling and seal well.

3. Tuck the parcels between hot coals or logs to cook. It will take 1–2 hours, depending on the intensity of the fire. Rotate the parcel several times during cooking, so the potatoes cook evenly.

4. Carefully open the parcels and serve scattered with the remaining coriander.

6.46. Quick & Easy Crispy Lamb Moroccan Rolls

(Serves 2, Cook Time 20 Minutes, Difficulty: Easy)

Ingredients:

- 250 g (8 oz) minced lamb
- 1 teaspoon ground cinnamon
- 3 tablespoons pine nuts
- 2 naan breads, warmed
- 200 g (7 oz) hummus
- 2 tablespoons mint leaves
- 1 Little Gem lettuce, finely shredded (optional)

Instructions:

1. Heat a frying pan until hot, add the minced lamb and fry for about 10 minutes until golden brown, breaking it up with a wooden spoon. Add the cinnamon and pine nuts and cook for a further 1 minute. Remove the lamb from the heat.

2. Place the warm naan bread on board using a rolling pin, firmly roll to flatten.

3. Mix the hummus with half the mint leaves, then spread in a thick layer over the naans. Spoon over the crispy lamb, then scatter the shredded lettuce, if using, and the remaining mint leaves.

4. Tightly roll up, cut in half, and serve, wrapped in foil if liked

6.47. Linguine with Shredded Ham & Eggs

(Serves 2, Cook Time 15 Minutes, Difficulty: Easy)

Ingredients:

- 3 tablespoons chopped flat leaf parsley
- 1 tablespoon coarse-grain mustard
- 2 teaspoons lemon juice
- good pinch of caster sugar
- 3 tablespoons olive oil
- 100 g (3½ oz) thinly sliced ham
- 2 spring onions
- 2 eggs
- 125 g (4 oz) dried linguine
- salt and pepper

Instructions:

1. Mix the parsley, mustard, lemon juice, sugar, oil, and a little salt and pepper in a bowl and set aside. Roll up the ham and slice it as thinly as possible. Trim the spring onions, cut them lengthways into thin shreds, then cut into 5 cm (2 inches) lengths.

2. Put the eggs in a small saucepan and cover with cold water. Bring to the boil and cook for 4 minutes (once the water boils, the eggs will usually start to move around).

3. Meanwhile, cook the pasta in a saucepan of salted water for 6–8 minutes, or until just tender. Add the spring onions and cook for a further 30 seconds.

4. Drain the pasta and return to the pan. Stir in the ham and the mustard dressing and pile on to plates. Shell and halve the eggs and serve on top.

6.48. Meatballs, Peas & Pasta

(Serves 4, Cook Time 20 Minutes, Difficulty: Normal)

Ingredients:

- 500 g (1 lb) beef or pork sausages, skins removed
- 4 tablespoons olive oil
- 400 g (13 oz) dried fusilli
- 250 g (8 oz) fresh peas, shelled
- 2 garlic cloves, sliced
- 2 tablespoons chopped sage
- ½ teaspoon dried chilli flakes
- salt and pepper
- grated Parmesan cheese, to serve

Instructions:

1. Cut the sausage meat into small pieces and roll into walnut-sized meatballs. Heat half the oil in a frying pan, add the meatballs, and cook over medium heat, frequently stirring, for about 10 minutes, or until cooked through. Transfer to a plate, cover with foil, and keep warm.

2. Meanwhile, cook the pasta in a large saucepan of lightly salted boiling water for 6 minutes. Add the peas, return to the boil, cook for a further 4 minutes, or wait until the peas and pasta are just tender. Drain well, reserving 4-tablespoons of the cooking water, then return to the pan.

3. Add the garlic, sage, chili flakes, salt, and pepper to taste to the meatball pan and cook over low heat for 2–3 minutes until the garlic is soft but not browned. Stir in the meatballs.

4. Tip the meatball mixture, reserved cooking water, and remaining oil into the pasta pan and heat through. Serve topped with grated Parmesan.

6.49. Pappardelle with Figs, Gorgonzola & Parma Ham

(Serves 4, Cook Time 5-10 Minutes, Difficulty: Normal)

Ingredients:

- 200 g (7 oz) fresh or dried pappardelle
- 2 tablespoons clear honey
- 2 teaspoons coarse-grain mustard
- 3 tablespoons orange juice
- squeeze of lemon juice
- 3 tablespoons olive oil
- 4 ripe, juicy figs, cut into thin wedges
- 100 g (3½ oz) Parma ham, torn into small pieces
- 150 g (5 oz) Gorgonzola cheese, roughly diced
- salt and pepper

Instructions:

1. Cook the pasta in a large saucepan of salted boiling water for 2–3 minutes for fresh and 8–10 minutes for dried.

2. Meanwhile, whisk together the honey, mustard, orange and lemon juice, oil, and a little salt and pepper in a bowl.

3. Drain the pasta and return it to the saucepan. Gently mix in the figs, ham, and Gorgonzola. Serve with the dressing spooned over.

6.50. Cheesy Turkey & Cranberry Melt

(Serves 4, Cook Time 20 Minutes, Difficulty: Normal)

Ingredients:

- 4 flat rolls

- 2 tablespoons wholegrain mustard
- 2 tablespoons cranberry sauce
- 200 g (7 oz) cooked turkey breast, sliced
- 125 g (4 oz) Cheddar cheese, grated

Instructions:

1. Split the rolls and spread half with the mustard and the other half with the cranberry sauce. Top with the turkey slices and cheese and sandwich together.

2. Heat a dry frying pan until hot, add 2-sandwiches and cook over medium-high heat for 4 minutes on each side until golden and the cheese has melted. Serve hot.

3. Repeat with the remaining 2-sandwiches.

6.51. Jamaican Spiced Salmon with Corn & Okra

(Serves 4, Cook Time 15 Minutes, Difficulty: Normal)

Ingredients:

- 4 skinless salmon fillets, about 175 g (6 oz) each
- 1 tablespoon Jamaican jerk seasoning
- 4 corn on the cobs, halved
- 3 tablespoons olive oil
- 1 red onion, sliced
- 250 g (8 oz) okra, trimmed
- 4 tablespoons butter
- ½ teaspoon paprika
- ½ teaspoon ground nutmeg
- salt

Instructions:

1. Rub each of the salmon fillets with the Jamaican jerk seasoning and set aside.

2. Cook the corn in a large saucepan of boiling water for about 5 minutes, or until tender. Drain well.

3. Heat 2 tablespoons of the oil in a large saucepan, add the onion and cook over medium heat, frequently stirring, for 2 minutes. Add the okra and cook, frequently stirring, for about a further 4 minutes until beginning to soften. Add the corn on the cobs to the pan with the butter and spices and toss for a further 2–3 minutes until lightly browned in places.

4. Meanwhile, heat the remaining tablespoon of oil in a frying pan and cook the salmon fillets, spice side down, over medium heat for 3–4 minutes, then turn over and cook for a further 2 minutes, or until cooked through. Serve hot with the corn and okra mixture.

6.52. Tuna Quesadilla with Salsa
(Serves 2, Cook Time 4-10 Minutes, Difficulty: Easy)

Ingredients:

- 2 soft flour tortillas
- 4 tablespoons ready-made fresh tomato salsa
- 2 spring onions, roughly chopped
- 75 g (3 oz) canned tuna, drained
- 50 g (2 oz) canned sweetcorn with peppers, drained
- 75 g (3 oz) mozzarella cheese, grated
- olive oil, for brushing

Instructions:

1. Place 1-tortilla on a plate and spread with the salsa. Sprinkle with the spring onions, tuna, sweetcorn, and cheese. Place the second tortilla on top and press down.

2. Heat a frying pan and brush with oil. Place the quesadilla in the pan and cook over medium heat for 2–3 minutes, pressing down with a spatula until the cheese starts to melt.

3. Place an inverted plate over the pan and turn the pan and plate together to tip the quesadilla onto the plate. Slide back into the pan and cook for 2–3 minutes on the other side. Serve cut into wedges.

6.53. Pesto & Salmon Pasta

(Serves 4, Cook Time 15 Minutes, Difficulty: Normal)

Ingredients:

- 325 g (11 oz) dried penne
- 2 tablespoons olive oil
- 1 onion, thinly sliced
- 400 g (13 oz) canned salmon
- 150 g (5 oz) fresh peas, shelled
- 2 tablespoons ready-made pesto
- 1 tablespoon lemon juice
- 25 g (1 oz) Parmesan cheese, grated, plus extra to serve
- salt and pepper
- leafy salad, to serve

Instructions:

1. Cook the pasta for about 8 minutes, or until almost tender, in a large saucepan of lightly salted boiling water.

2. After that, heat the oil in a frying pan, add the onion and cook until softened, about 5 minutes over medium heat.

3. Drain the salmon and discard the bones and meat. Flake the flesh. Apply the peas to the pasta and simmer until just tender, for a further 5 minutes. Drain the pasta and peas,

maintain the cooking water for a few teaspoons, and return to the pan.

4. Pesto, lemon juice, parmesan cheese, onion, reserved water, and flaked salmon are added. With salt and pepper, season lightly and toss gently. Serve with extra Parmesan cheese and a leafy salad.

6.54. Pasta Salad with Crab, Lime & Rocket

(Serves 2, Cook Time 10 Minutes, Difficulty: Normal)

Ingredients:

- 50 g (2 oz) dried pasta (such as rigatoni)
- grated rind and juice of ½ a lime
- 2 tablespoons crème fraîche
- 85 g (3¼ oz) canned crab meat, drained
- 8 cherry tomatoes, halved
- handful of rocket leaves

Instructions:

1. Cook the pasta in a saucepan of boiling water for about 10 minutes, or until tender, then drain and leave to cool.

2. Mix the lime rind and juice, crème fraîche, and crab meat in a large bowl. Add the pasta and mix again.

3. Add the tomatoes and rocket to the bowl, toss everything together and serve.

6.55. Prawn, Mango & Avocado Wrap

(Serves 2, Cook Time 20 Minutes, Difficulty: Normal)

Ingredients:

- 2 tablespoons crème fraîche
- 2 teaspoons tomato ketchup

- few drops of Tabasco sauce
- 300 g (10 oz) cooked peeled prawns
- 1 mango, peeled, stoned and thinly sliced
- 1 avocado, peeled, stoned and sliced
- 100 g (3½ oz) watercress
- 4 flour tortillas

Instructions:

1. Mix the crème fraîche and ketchup. Add a few drops of Tabasco sauce to taste. Add the prawns, mango, and avocado, and toss the mixture together.

2. Divide the mixture among the tortillas, add some watercress, then roll up and serve.

6.56. Griddled Greek-Style Sandwiches

(Serves 2, Cook Time 15 Minutes, Difficulty: Normal)

Ingredients:

- ¼ small red onion, thinly sliced
- 8 cherry tomatoes, quartered
- 4 pitted black olives, chopped
- 5 cm (2 inch) piece of cucumber, deseeded and cut into small pieces
- 1 teaspoon dried oregano
- 50 g (2 oz) feta cheese, crumbled
- 1 teaspoon lemon juice
- 2 round seeded pitta breads
- 25 g (1 oz) Cheddar cheese, grated
- olive oil, for brushing
- pepper

Instructions:

1. Mix the onion, tomatoes, olives, cucumber, oregano, and feta in a small bowl. Add the lemon juice, season to taste with pepper, and mix gently.

2. Split each pitta bread in half horizontally. Divide the feta mixture between the bottom halves of the pitta bread, then add the Cheddar.

3. Cover with the top halves of the pitta bread.

4. Brush a griddle pan or frying pan with oil and heat over medium heat. When hot, add the sandwiches, press down gently with a spatula, and cook for about 2–3 minutes on each side, or until golden and the cheese has melted. Serve immediately

---

6.57. Mediterranean Goats' Cheese Omelettes

(Serves 2, Cook Time 30 Minutes, Difficulty: Normal)

Ingredients:

- 50 ml (2 Fl oz) olive oil
- 500 g (1 lb) cherry tomatoes, halved
- a little chopped basil
- 12 eggs
- 2 tablespoons wholegrain mustard
- 4 tablespoons butter
- 125 g (4 oz) soft goats' cheese, diced
- salt and pepper

Instructions:

1. Heat the oil in a frying pan, add the tomatoes and fry for 2–3 minutes until they have softened – if necessary, do this in two batches. Add the basil and season with salt and pepper, then transfer to a bowl, cover with foil and keep warm.

2. Beat the eggs with the mustard in a bowl and season with salt and pepper. Melt a

quarter of the butter in a frying pan, then swirl in a quarter of the egg mixture. Fork over the omelet so that it cooks evenly.

3. As soon as it is set on the bottom (but still a little runny in the middle), dot over a quarter of the goats' cheese and cook for a further 30 seconds.

4. Carefully slide the omelet onto a plate, folding it in half as you do so, and serve with a quarter of the tomatoes.

5. Repeat with the remaining mixture to make 3-more omelets, and serve with the remaining tomatoes.

6.58. Caramelized Onion & Cheese Crêpes
(Serves 4, Cook Time 20-30 Minutes, Difficulty: Normal)

Ingredients:

- 150 g (5 oz) whole meal flour
- pinch of salt
- 1 egg, lightly beaten
- 300 ml (½ pint) milk
- 1 tablespoon mustard
- vegetable oil, for frying

Filling

- 3 tablespoons butter
- 3 onions, thinly sliced
- 2 teaspoons caster sugar
- a few thyme sprigs
- 250 g (8 oz) Emmental or Gruyère cheese, grated
- salt and pepper

Instructions:

1. Put the flour and salt in a bowl and make a well in the center. Pour the egg and some of the milk into the well, then beat, gradually incorporating the flour to smooth paste. Beat in the remaining milk and the mustard. Set aside.

2. To make the filling, melt the butter in a saucepan, add the onions and sugar, cook over low heat for about 10–15 minutes, or be softened, deep golden, and caramelized. Tear the thyme leaves off the stems and add them to the pan with salt and plenty of pepper. Remove from the heat and keep warm.

3. Heat a little oil in a frying pan until it starts to smoke, then pour off the excess into a cup. Pour a quarter of the batter into the pan, tilting it until the bottom is coated with a thin layer. Cook for 1–2 minutes, or until golden underneath. Carefully flip the crêpe over and cook for a further 30–45 seconds until it is golden on the other side.

4. Add a quarter of the onions and cheese to one half of the crêpe and heat briefly until the cheese begins to melt, then flip over and slide on to a plate. Serve immediately.

5. Repeat with the remaining batter and filling to make three more crêpes, adding a little more oil to the pan as required.

6.59. Sweetcorn Fritters with Sweet Chilli Dip

(Serves 4, Cook Time 20 Minutes, Difficulty: Normal)

Ingredients:

- 250 g (8 oz) plain flour
- 2 eggs
- 125 ml (4 Fl oz) milk
- 6 spring onions, chopped
- 2 x 325 g (11 oz) cans sweetcorn, drained well
- 2 tablespoons vegetable oil, plus extra if required
- salt and pepper

- fresh coriander leaves, to garnish
- Sweet chilly dip
- 250 g (8 oz) light soft cheese
- 2 tablespoons sweet chilly sauce

Instructions:

1. Place the flour in a bowl and make a well in the center. Break the eggs into the well and add the milk. Gradually whisk the flour into the eggs and milk to make a smooth, thick batter. Stir in the spring onions and sweetcorn and season with salt and pepper.

2. Make the dip, put the soft cheese in a bowl and stir to soften, then lightly stir through the sweet chili sauce to form a marbled effect. Heat the oil in a frying pan, add spoonfuls of the batter, about four at a time, cook for 2-minutes on each side until golden, firm to the touch, and heated through. Serve the fritters warm with the dip, sprinkled with coriander leaves.

3. Repeat with the remaining batter, adding extra oil if necessary.

6.60. Lemon, Ricotta & Courgette Ribbon
(Serves 4, Cook Time 15 Minutes, Difficulty: Normal)

Ingredients:

- stir-fry
- 250 g (8 oz) dried parpardelle or tagliatelle
- 400 g (13 oz) small baby courgettes
- salt and pepper
- green salad, to serve
- Lemony ricotta
- 1 teaspoon fennel seeds
- ¼ teaspoon dried chilly flakes (optional)
- 12–15 black peppercorns
- 250 g (8 oz) ricotta cheese

- ¼ teaspoon ground nutmeg
- finely grated rind and juice of 1 lemon

Instructions:

1. To make the lemony ricotta, lightly crush the fennel seeds with the chili flakes, if using, and black peppercorns, then tip into a bowl. Add the ricotta, nutmeg, lemon rind, and juice and mix well, then set aside.

2. Cook the pasta in a saucepan of boiling water for about 5 minutes, or until just tender.

3. Meanwhile, slice the courgettes thinly into ribbons using a sharp vegetable peeler.

4. Add the courgettes to the pasta and cook for a further 2 minutes, or until the pasta is tender and the courgettes softened.

5. Drain the pasta and courgettes, reserving 2–3 tablespoons of the cooking liquid. Return the pasta, courgettes, and reserved water to the pan, add the lemony ricotta and stir gently to combine. Season with salt and pepper, then serve with a green salad.

6.61. Curried Cauliflower, Lentil & Rice

(Serves 4, Cook Time 30 Minutes, Difficulty: Normal)

Ingredients:

- 2 tablespoons vegetable oil
- 1 large onion, sliced
- 2 teaspoons cumin seeds
- 2 tablespoons Jalfrezi curry paste 350 g
- (11½ oz) cauliflower, cut into
- florets 100 g
- (3½ oz) red lentils, rinsed 150 g
- (5 oz) basmati rice 700 ml
- (1¼ pints) hot vegetable stock

- 2 carrots, coarsely grated 50 g
- (2 oz) toasted cashew nuts
- 2 handfuls of fresh coriander leaves, to garnish

Instructions:

1. Heat the oil in a frying pan, add the onion and cook over medium heat for about 5 minutes until softened. Add the cumin seeds and cook for 30 seconds, then add the curry paste and cook for a further 30 seconds.

2. Add the cauliflower, red lentils, rice, and stock and bring to the boil, then cover with a lid and simmer gently for 10–15 minutes, or until cooked through and the liquid is absorbed.

3. Stir in the grated carrots and cook for 2 minutes, adding a little hot water if the mixture is too dry. Sprinkle over the cashews and serve scattered with coriander leaves.

6.62. Big Mac 'N' Cheese

(Serves 4, Cook Time 20 Minutes, Difficulty: Normal)

Ingredients:

- 250 g (8 oz) macaroni
- pinch of ground nutmeg
- 4 tablespoons butter
- 30 g (1 oz) plain flour
- 600 ml (1 pint) milk
- 2 teaspoons Dijon mustard
- 200 g (7 oz) grated Cheddar cheese
- 4 small tomatoes, cut into wedges
- salt and pepper

Instructions:

1. Cook the macaroni in a large saucepan of boiling water for 10–12 minutes, or until tender.

2. Drain the pasta. Dry the saucepan, then add the butter and heat until melted. Stir in the flour, then gradually add the milk and bring to the boil, continually stirring, until thickened.

3. Stir in the mustard, cheese, and plenty of salt and pepper and heat until the cheese has melted. Stir in the macaroni and tomatoes and heat through.

6.63. Green Cheese Pasta

(Serves 4, Cook Time 15 Minutes, Difficulty: Normal)

Ingredients:

- 250 g (8 oz) dried pasta shapes
- 300 g (10 oz) spinach leaves
- 1 teaspoon ground nutmeg
- 4 tablespoons butter
- 50 g (2 oz) plain flour
- 600 ml (1 pint) milk
- 100 g (4 oz) Cheddar cheese, grated

Instructions:

1. Cook the pasta shapes for 8–10 minutes in a saucepan of boiling water, or until just tender. Drain and set aside.

2. Meanwhile, rinse the spinach with water and roughly drain, then cook in a hot frying pan for about 2 minutes until just wilted. Press out any water and chop finely, then return to the pan and toss with the nutmeg. Set aside.

3. Melt the butter in a saucepan. Remove from the heat, add the flour and stir to form a thick paste. Return to the heat and cook gently for a few seconds, stirring constantly.

4. Remove from the heat and gradually add the milk, stirring well after each addition. Return to the heat and bring to the boil, continually stirring until the sauce has boiled and thickened. Add the spinach, cheese, and pasta, stir well to coat, and heat through gently.

6.64. Refried Bean Quesadilla

(Serves 2, Cook Time 10-15 Minutes, Difficulty: Normal)

Ingredients:

- 200 g (7 oz) canned refried beans
- 2 spring onions, chopped
- 50 g (2 oz) canned sweetcorn, drained
- 1 tablespoon chopped fresh coriander
- 2 soft corn tortillas
- 3 tablespoons ready-made fresh tomato salsa, plus extra to serve
- 50 g (2 oz) Cheddar or Monterey Jack cheese, grated
- olive oil, for brushing

Instructions:

1. Mix the refried beans, spring onions, sweetcorn, and coriander in a bowl.

2. Spread 1-tortilla with the bean mixture, top with the salsa, and sprinkle over the cheese. Cover with the remaining tortilla.

3. Brush a frying pan or griddle pan with oil and heat over medium heat. When hot, add the quesadilla and cook over medium heat for 2–3 minutes, pressing down with a spatula, until the cheese starts to melt.

4. Place a large plate over the pan and turn the quesadilla over on to the plate. Return to the pan and cook for 2–3 minutes on the other side. Cut into wedges and serve with extra tomato salsa.

6.65. Orzo Risotto with Pancetta & Peas

(Serves 4, Cook Time 10-15 Minutes, Difficulty: Normal)

Ingredients:

- 900 ml (1½ pints) hot chicken or vegetable stock
- 350 g (11½ oz) orzo pasta
- a knob of butter
- 1 teaspoon chopped garlic
- 150 g (5 oz) diced pancetta
- 200 g (7 oz) fresh peas, shelled
- handful of parsley, chopped
- 75 g (3 oz) Parmesan cheese, grated
- salt and pepper

Instructions:

1. Place the stock in a saucepan, bring to the boil and add the pasta. Meanwhile, melt the butter in a small frying pan until foaming, add the garlic and pancetta and fry for 2 minutes, or until the pancetta is crispy.

2. Add the pancetta and garlic to the orzo with the peas and continue to cook over medium heat for about 7 minutes, or until the pasta and peas are just tender, occasionally stirring to prevent the pasta from sticking and adding a little more water if necessary.

3. Season to taste with salt and pepper and stir in the parsley and most of the Parmesan. Serve immediately, sprinkled with the remaining Parmesan and freshly ground black pepper

Chapter 7: Camping Sides; Salads, Sauces & Snacks Recipes

In this chapter, we will provide you amazing and healthy Side Recipes, Salad Recipes, Sauces Recipes and Snacks Recipes that you can cook while camping.

7.1. Sardines on Rye

(Serves 3, Cook Time 10 Minutes, Difficulty: Easy)

Ingredients:

- 250 g (8 oz) can sardine in oil, drained
- 125 g (4 oz) cream cheese
- 2 tablespoons grated cucumber, drained
- 1 spring onion, finely chopped
- 6 thin slices of rye bread
- butter, for spreading
- lettuce leaves

Instructions:

1. In a bowl, bring the sardines and cream cheese and mix them around. Stir in the

cucumber and the onion for the season.

2. Spread the butter with 3-slices of the rye bread, add the mixture of sardines and lettuce, and top with the additional slices of bread.

7.2. Spiced Mackerel Fillets

(Serves 4, Cook Time 10 Minutes, Difficulty: Easy)

Ingredients:

- 2 tablespoons olive oil
- 1 tablespoon smoked paprika
- 1 teaspoon cayenne
- pepper
- 8 fresh mackerel fillets.
- 2 limes, quartered salt and pepper rocket
- salad, to serve

Instructions:

1. In a bowl, add the oil, paprika, and cayenne together and season with salt and pepper to taste. Require three shallow cuts of each mackerel fillet on the skin and spread the spiced oil all over.

2. Over a hot barbecue or campfire, cook the lime quarters and mackerel fillets on a grill plate, skin side down, for about 5 minutes, or until the skin is crispy, and the limes are charred. Turn the fish over and cook for the next 1 minute or until cooked thoroughly.

3. Serve with a rocket salad.

7.3. Eggs Florentine

(Serves 4, Cook Time 15 Minutes, Difficulty: Easy)

Ingredients:

- a knob of butter, plus extra for spreading
- 200 g (7 oz) spinach leaves
- 4 muffins
- 3 tablespoons chopped parsley
- 200 ml (7 Fl oz) jar hollandaise sauce
- salt and pepper
- 4 eggs
- 1 tablespoon vinegar

Ingredients:

1. In a large saucepan, melt the butter, add the spinach and simmer over medium heat, stirring, until wilted for 1–2 minutes. Use salt and pepper to season, cover with a cap, and stay warm.

2. Split the muffins and toast until finely burnt, cut side down, in a griddle pan or over a grill or campfire. Cover and hold warm in a clean tea towel. In a tub, mix the parsley and hollandaise sauce.

3. Meanwhile, to the boil, put a big saucepan of water. In a cup, split 1 of the eggs, making sure not to break the yolk. Apply the vinegar to the boiling water, and instantly stir the water to make a whirlpool in a circular motion. Slide the egg into the middle of the pan gently while the water is still swirling, keeping the cup as tightly as you can to the water. Cook for 1-2 minutes, or until the white is trustworthy, then raise out with a slotted spoon, and the yolk is tender.

4. Then add a fifth of the spinach and finish with an egg—butter 2-halves of a muffin. Spoon and serve with freshly ground black pepper over the hollandaise sauce.

5. Cook and serve the other 3-eggs in the same manner, each time before slipping into the shell, stirring the boiling water into a whirlpool.

7.4. Smoked Mackerel Pasta Salad

(Serves 4, Cook Time 20-25 Minutes, Difficulty: Easy)

Ingredients:

- 300 g (10 oz) dried conchiglie pasta
- 200 g (7 oz) green beans, trimmed
- 4 hot-smoked peppered boneless mackerel fillets
- 125 g (4 oz) mixed salad
- ½ cucumber, cut in half lengthways, deseeded and cut into chunky pieces
- 2 spring onions, finely sliced
- 2 hard-boiled eggs, quartered

Dressing

- 100 ml (3½ Fl oz) soured cream
- 1 tablespoon wholegrain mustard
- 1 teaspoon French mustard
- 2 tablespoons lemon juice
- 1 teaspoon chopped dill
- 1 teaspoon chopped tarragon
- salt and pepper

Instructions:

1. Cook the pasta in a large saucepan of lightly salted boiling water for about 10–12 minutes, or until just tender. Drain and leave to cool.

2. Meanwhile, cook the beans in a saucepan of lightly salted boiling water for about 5 minutes, or until just tender. Drain and leave to cool.

3. To make the dressing, mix all the ingredients in a small bowl and season with salt and pepper.

4. Tip the pasta into a large bowl, then flake the smoked mackerel fillets into the bowl. Add the salad leaves, cucumber, spring onions, cooled beans, and then toss with some of the dressing.

5. Divide the pasta salad among serving bowls and top with the hard-boiled 5-eggs. Serve with the dressing

7.5. Seared Tuna with Bean & Rocket Salad

(Serves 4, Cook Time 20 Minutes, Difficulty: Easy)

Ingredients:

- 4 tablespoons olive oil
- 4 tuna steaks, about 150 g (5 oz) each
- 2–4 tablespoons lemon juice
- finely grated rind of ½ lemon
- 2 x 400 g (13 oz) cans cannellini beans, drained
- 100 g (3½ oz) rocket leaves
- 1 small red onion, finely sliced
- 1 red chilly, deseeded and chopped
- salt and pepper

Instructions:

1. Rub 1-tablespoon of the oil and season very well salt and pepper over the tuna steaks. Heat a griddle pan until it is hot to smoke, then cook the tuna on either side for 1-2 minutes or crispy in the center on the outside but still pink. Cook for a little less or longer, instead, until baked to your liking.

2. After that, add 2-teaspoons of the lemon juice with the remaining oil and season with salt and pepper to taste in a bowl. In a wide tub, toss with the remaining ingredients and add more lemon juice to taste.

3. With the seared tuna, serve the bean salad.

7.6. Herbed Lamb with Fig Salad

(Serves 4, Cook Time 10 Minutes, Difficulty: Easy)

Ingredients:

- 2 tablespoons coriander seeds
- 2 tablespoons chopped rosemary
- grated rind of 1 lemon
- salt and black pepper
- 100 ml (3½ Fl oz) olive oil
- 1 garlic clove, crushed
- 12 lamb cutlets
- 125 g (4 oz) rocket leaves
- 4 figs, sliced
- 75 g (3 oz) pitted black olives, halved
- 2–3 teaspoons lemon juice, to taste
- yogurt, to serve

Instructions:

1. To make the rub, dry-fry the coriander seeds in a frying pan over high heat for 2–3 minutes until they begin to pop and release their aroma.

2. Cool the coriander seeds, mix them with rosemary, lemon rind, and salt and pepper.

3. Put 2-tablespoons of the oil, the rub, the garlic, and some salt and pepper in a large sealable plastic bag. Add the lamb, toss well and seal the bag.

4. Leave to marinate in a cool box for 1–4 hours.

5. Remove the lamb from the marinade and pat dry. Transfer to a grill rack over a hot barbecue or campfire and cook for about 2–3 minutes on each side, or until cooked to your liking, then wrap loosely with foil and leave to rest for 5 minutes.

6. Meanwhile, to make the salad, put the rocket, figs, and olives in a large bowl and mix well. Whisk together the remaining oil and 2–3 teaspoons lemon juice with some salt and pepper. Add to the salad and stir to coat the leaves. Serve with the lamb and some yogurt.

7.7. Cypriot Chicken & Haloumi Salad

(Serves 4, Cook Time 25 Minutes, Difficulty: Easy)

Ingredients:

- 3 boneless, skinless chicken breast fillets, about 125 g (4 oz) each
- 1 bunch of oregano, chopped
- 1 tablespoon olive oil
- 250 g (8 oz) haloumi cheese
- salt and pepper
- Cypriot salad
- 1 cucumber, skinned, deseeded and cut lengthways into short batons
- 4 large tomatoes, skinned, deseeded and cut into wedges
- 1 red onion, finely chopped
- 1 bunch of flat leaf parsley, roughly chopped
- 3 tablespoons olive oil
- 1 tablespoon wine vinegar

Instructions:

1. Put the chicken in a bowl, stir in the chopped oregano, olive oil, salt, and pepper, and

blend well. Fill with clingfilm and leave for 2 hours in a cool box to marinate.

2. Switch chicken over a campfire to grill rack and cook on either side for around 6–8 minutes, or until cooked through.

3. Swap to a tray, break into pieces, cover, and stay warm with foil. Meanwhile, bring the cucumber, tomato wedges, sliced red onion, and parsley into a bowl to make the salad. Add the wine vinegar and olive oil, toss well and season with salt and pepper to taste.

4. Slice the halloumi into 8 bits, then move them to the grill rack and cook on each side for about 4 minutes. Serve with the salad and chicken.

7.8. Chickpea & Herb Salad

(Serves 4, Cook Time 20 Minutes, Difficulty: Easy)

Ingredients:

- 100 g (3½ oz) bulgar wheat
- 4 tablespoons olive oil
- 1 tablespoon lemon juice
- 2 tablespoons chopped flat leaf parsley
- 1 tablespoon chopped mint 400 g
- (13 oz) can chickpeas, drained
- 125 g (4 oz) cherry tomatoes, halved
- 1 tablespoon chopped mild onion
- 100 g (3½ oz) cucumber, diced
- 150 g (5 oz) feta cheese, diced salt and pepper

Instructions:

1. Put the bulgar wheat in a heatproof bowl and cover with boiling water. Leave to stand until the water is absorbed, then drain well, pressing out as much moisture as possible with the back of a spoon. Leave to cool.

2. Mix the oil, lemon juice, parsley, mint, salt, and pepper in a large bowl. Add the chickpeas, tomatoes, onion, cucumber, and bulgar wheat. Mix well, then add the feta, stirring lightly to avoid breaking up the cheese.

7.9. Orange & Avocado Salad

(Serves 4, Cook Time 15 Minutes, Difficulty: Easy)

Ingredients:

- 4 large juicy oranges
- 2 small ripe avocados, peeled and stoned
- 2 teaspoons cardamom pods
- 3 tablespoons olive oil
- 1 tablespoon clear honey
- pinch of ground allspice
- 2 teaspoons lemon juice
- salt and pepper
- sprigs of watercress, to garnish

Instructions:

1. Using a sharp knife, remove the peel and pith from the oranges over a bowl to catch the juice, cut between the membranes to remove the segments. Slice the avocados and toss gently with the orange segments. Pile into serving bowls.

2. Reserve a few whole cardamom pods for garnishing. Crush the remainder using a pestle and mortar to extract the seeds or place them in a small bowl and crush with the end of a rolling pin. Pick out and discard the pods.

3. Mix the seeds with the oil, honey, allspice, and lemon juice in a bowl.

4. Season to taste with salt and pepper and stir in the reserved orange juice.

5. Garnish the salads with watercress sprigs and the reserved cardamom pods and serve with the dressing spooned over the top.

7.10. Ribboned Carrot Salad

(Serves 4, Cook Time 20 Minutes, Difficulty: Easy)

Ingredients:

- 4 carrots
- 2 celery sticks
- 1 bunch of spring onions
- 4 tablespoons olive oil
- 2 tablespoons lime juice
- 2 teaspoons caster sugar
- ¼ teaspoon dried chilly flakes
- 2 tablespoons chopped mint
- 50 g (2 oz) salted peanuts
- salt and pepper

Instructions:

1. Half fill a medium bowl with freezing water, adding a few ice cubes if possible.

2. Scrub the carrots and pare off as many long ribbons as you can from each. Place the ribbons in the water. Cut the celery into 5 cm (2 inches) lengths. Cut each length into skinny slices. Cut the spring onions into 5 cm (2 inches) lengths and shred lengthways.

3. Add the celery and spring onions to the water and leave to soak for 15–20 minutes until the vegetables curl up.

4. Mix the oil, lime juice, sugar, chili flakes, and mint in a small bowl and season to taste with salt and pepper.

5. Thoroughly drain the vegetables and toss them in a bowl with the dressing, peanuts, salt, and pepper. Serve the salad immediately.

7.11. Griddled Haloumi with Warm Couscous Salad
(Serves 4, Cook Time 20 Minutes, Difficulty: Easy)

Ingredients:

- 5 tablespoons olive oil
- 2 red onions, thinly sliced
- 1 red chilly, roughly chopped
- 400 g (13 oz) can chickpeas, drained
- 175 g (6 oz) cherry tomatoes, halved
- 200 g (7 oz) couscous
- ½ teaspoon salt
- 3 tablespoons chopped parsley
- 1 tablespoon thyme leaves
- 375 g (12 oz) haloumi cheese, thickly sliced

Instructions:

1. Heat 3 tablespoons of the oil in a frying pan, add the onions and two-thirds of the chili and cook over medium heat, stirring, for about 5 minutes until softened. Add the chickpeas and tomatoes and cook over high heat for 3 minutes, occasionally stirring, until the chickpeas are heated through, and the tomatoes are softened but still retaining their shape.

2. Meanwhile, put the couscous in a heatproof bowl, add enough boiling water to cover by 1 cm (½ inch), and mix in the salt. Cover with clingfilm and leave to stand for 5 minutes, then fluff up with a fork.

3. Heat a griddle pan until hot. Mix the remaining olive oil and chili with the herbs in a shallow bowl. Add the halloumi slices and toss to coat, then transfer to the griddle pan and cook for about 2–3 minutes, turning once, until browned in places.

4. Stir the couscous into the chickpea mixture and cook for 1 minute to heat through—pile on to plates and top with the halloumi slices.

7.12. Egg, Basil & Cheese Salad with Cherry Tomatoes

(Serves 4, Cook Time 10 Minutes, Difficulty: Easy)

Ingredients:

- 2 tablespoons olive oil
- 2 eggs, beaten
- 2 handfuls of basil, roughly chopped
- 200 g (7 oz) feta cheese, crumbled
- 250 g (8 oz) cherry plum tomatoes, halved
- 80 g (3 oz) watercress
- 1 tablespoon balsamic vinegar
- pepper

Instructions:

1. Heat 1-tablespoon of the oil in a frying pan and swirl around. Beat the eggs in a large jug with the basil and plenty of pepper, then pour into the pan in a thin layer and cook for about 2-minutes, or until golden and set. Remove and cut into thick strips.

2. Meanwhile, toss the feta, cherry tomatoes, and watercress in a bowl. Mix the remaining oil with the balsamic vinegar, pour over the salad, and toss to coat.

3. Add the omelet strips, toss to mix, and serve while still warm.

7.13. Spicy Sweet Potato & Feta Salad

(Serves 4, Cook Time 15 Minutes, Difficulty: Easy)

Ingredients:

- 5 tablespoons olive oil
- 2 sweet potatoes, thinly sliced
- 1 tablespoon white wine vinegar
- 150 g (5 oz) baby spinach leaves
- 1 tablespoon finely chopped red onion
- 125 g (4 oz) feta cheese, crumbled
- 1 red chilly, sliced
- 50 g (2 oz) pitted black olives
- salt and pepper

Instructions:

1. Heat a griddle pan until hot. Toss together 2-tablespoons of the oil and the sweet potatoes in a bowl. Season well with salt and pepper, cook in the hot griddle pan for about 3 minutes on each side, or tender and lightly charred.

2. Meanwhile, mix the remaining oil and vinegar in a bowl and season to taste with salt and pepper. Add the spinach and onion and toss together.

3. Transfer the sweet potatoes to plates, top with the spinach and onion, feta, chili, olives, and serve.

7.14. Real Guacamole with raw vegetables

(Serves 4, Cook Time 10 Minutes, Difficulty: Easy)

Ingredients:

- 2 large firm, ripe avocados
- ½ small red onion, finely chopped

- 2 tablespoons lime juice
- 3 tablespoons finely chopped fresh coriander
- ¼ teaspoon garlic powder
- ¼ teaspoon celery salt
- pinch of cayenne pepper
- ½ teaspoon paprika
- 3 tomatoes, deseeded and finely chopped
- few dashes of Tabasco (optional)
- salt and pepper

To serve

- 350 g (11½ oz) carrots, cut into batons
- 350 g (11½ oz) cauliflower florets
- 4 celery sticks, cut into batons
- 250 g (8 oz) radishes, trimmed
- 125 g (4 oz) baby sweetcorn

Instructions:

1. Peel the avocados, remove the stones, and then mash the flesh in a small bowl with the back of a fork to break it up.

2. Add the red onion, lime juice, coriander, garlic powder, celery salt, and spices. Mix until almost smooth, with some small lumps, then season with salt and pepper. Stir in the tomatoes and add Tabasco, if using.

3. Arrange the raw vegetables on a large plate and serve with the guacamole.

7.15. Warm Courgette & Lime Salad

(Serves 4, Cook Time 15 Minutes, Difficulty: Easy)

Ingredients:

- 1 tablespoon olive oil
- grated rind and juice of 1 lime
- 1 garlic clove, finely chopped
- 2 tablespoons roughly chopped fresh coriander, plus extra to garnish
- 2 courgettes, about 325 g (11 oz) in total, cut into thin diagonal slices
- salt and pepper

Instructions:

1. Mix the oil, lime rind and juice, garlic, chopped coriander, salt, and pepper in a sealable plastic bag. Add the courgette slices and toss in the oil mixture. Seal and set aside until ready to cook.

2. Heat a griddle pan until hot. Arrange as many courgette slices as will fit in a single layer over the pan's base and cook for about 2–3 minutes, or until browned on the underside. Turn the slices over and brown on the other side. Transfer the slices to a serving dish, cover with foil, and keep warm. Repeat with the remaining courgettes.

3. Pour any remaining dressing over the courgettes, sprinkle with a little extra chopped coriander to garnish, and serve immediately.

7.16. Garlic Bread

(Serves 4, Cook Time 15 Minutes, Difficulty: Easy)

Ingredients:

- 4 tablespoons butter, softened
- 1 garlic clove, crushed
- 2 tablespoons thyme leaves, roughly chopped (optional)

- 1 white or wholemeal baguette
- salt and pepper

Instructions:

1. Beat the softened butter with the garlic and thyme, if using, in a bowl and season with a little salt and pepper. Cut the baguette into thick slices, almost all the way through but leaving the base attached. Spread the butter thickly over each slice.

2. Wrap the baguette in foil and cook on a grill rack over a barbecue or campfire for about 15 minutes, occasionally turning the parcel.

3. Alternatively, cook in a griddle pan on a camping stove.

7.17. Devilled Mushrooms

(Serves 4, Cook Time 15 Minutes, Difficulty: Easy)

Ingredients:

- 6 spring onions
- 4 tablespoons butter
- 1 tablespoon sunflower oil
- 425 g (14 oz) white mushrooms, sliced
- 2 tablespoons Worcestershire sauce
- 2 teaspoons wholegrain mustard
- 2 teaspoons tomato paste
- a few drops of Tabasco sauce (optional)
- 4 slices of crusty bread
- salt and pepper

Instructions:

1. Finely chop the spring onions, reserving the green tops. Heat the butter and oil in a frying pan, add the white chopped spring onions and the mushrooms, and fry, stirring, for

about 3–4 minutes, or until golden.

2. Stir in the Worcestershire sauce, mustard, and tomato paste. Add 4 tablespoons of water, Tabasco, if using, and a little salt and pepper and cook for 2 minutes, stirring, until the sauce is beginning to thicken.

3. After that, toast the bread on both sides in a griddle pan or on a rack over a barbecue or campfire. Transfer to plates.

4. Stir the green spring onion tops through the mushrooms, cook for 1 minute, and then spoon over the toast and serve.

7.18. Tabbouleh with Fruit & Nuts

(Serves 4, Cook Time 10 Minutes, Difficulty: Easy)

Ingredients:

- 150 g (5 oz) bulgar wheat
- 75 g (3 oz) unsalted, shelled pistachio nuts
- 1 small red onion, finely chopped
- 3 garlic cloves, crushed
- 2 handfuls of flat leaf parsley, chopped
- large handful of mint, chopped
- finely grated rind and juice of 1 lemon or lime
- 150 g (5 oz) ready-to-eat prunes, sliced
- 4 tablespoons olive oil
- salt and pepper

Instructions:

1. Put the bulgar wheat in a heatproof bowl and cover with plenty of boiling water. Leave to stand for 15 minutes.

2. Meanwhile, mix the pistachios, onion, garlic, parsley, mint, lemon or lime rind, juice, and prunes in a large bowl.

3. Drain the bulgar wheat well, pressing out as much moisture as possible with the back of a spoon. Add to the other ingredients with the oil and toss together.

4. Season to taste with salt and pepper and serve.

7.19. Green Couscous with Spiced Fruit Sauce
(Serves 4, Cook Time 20 Minutes, Difficulty: Easy)

Ingredients:

- 500 ml (17 Fl oz) hot vegetable stock
- 250 g (8 oz) couscous
- 75 g (3 oz) unsalted, shelled pistachio nuts, roughly chopped
- 2 spring onions, chopped
- small handful of parsley, chopped
- 425 g (14 oz) can flageolet beans, drained
- salt and pepper
- Spiced fruit sauce
- ½ teaspoon saffron threads
- 1 tablespoon cardamom pods
- 2 teaspoons coriander seeds
- ½ teaspoon chilly powder
- 4 tablespoons flaked almonds
- 75 g (3 oz) ready-to-eat dried apricots, finely chopped

Instructions:

1. To make the sauce, put the saffron in a small cup and pour over 1-tablespoon boiling water. Leave to stand for 3 minutes.

2. Crush the cardamom pods using a pestle and mortar, or place them in a small bowl and crush with the end of a rolling pin. Pick out and discard the pods, then lightly crush the seeds.

3. Add the coriander seeds, chili powder, and almonds to the bowl and crush again. Stir in the apricots. Pour in the saffron and soaking liquid and 200 ml (7 Fl oz) of the hot stock, season with salt and pepper, and mix well. Transfer to a saucepan and heat through.

4. Meanwhile, put the couscous in a heatproof bowl and add the remaining hot stock.

Cover with clingfilm and leave to stand for 5 minutes until the stock is absorbed, then fluff up with a fork. Stir in the pistachios, spring onions, parsley, and beans, and season to taste with salt and pepper. Serve with the fruit sauce.

7.20. Thai-dressed Tofu Rolls

(Serves 4, Cook Time 15 Minutes, Difficulty: Easy)

Ingredients:

- 1 small iceberg lettuce
- 275 g (9 oz) tofu, diced
- 100 g (3½ oz) mangetout, shredded lengthways
- 2 tablespoons olive oil
- 2 tablespoons light soy sauce
- 2 tablespoons lime juice
- 1 tablespoon muscovado sugar
- 1 Thai chilly, deseeded and sliced
- 1 garlic clove, crushed

- pepper

Instructions:

1. Remove 8-leaves from the lettuce. Fill a large heatproof bowl with boiling water. Add the separated leaves and leave for 10 seconds. Rinse in cold water and drain well.

2. Finely shred the remaining lettuce and toss in a bowl with the tofu and mangetout.

3. Mix the oil, soy sauce, lime juice, sugar, chili, garlic, and pepper in a separate bowl and add to the tofu mixture. Toss together gently, using two spoons.

4. Spoon a little mixture on to the center of each blanched lettuce leaf, then roll up and serve.

7.21. Tortillas with chilly & aubergine yogurt

(Serves 2, Cook Time 20 Minutes, Difficulty: Easy)

Ingredients:

- 4 tablespoons olive oil
- 1 aubergine, thinly sliced
- small handful of mint, chopped
- small handful of parsley, chopped
- 2 tablespoons chopped chives
- 1 green chilly, deseeded and thinly sliced
- 200 ml (7 Fl oz) Greek yogurt
- 2 tablespoons mayonnaise
- 2 large tortillas
- 7 cm (3 inch) length of cucumber, thinly sliced
- salt and pepper
- paprika, to garnish

Instructions:

1. Heat the oil in a frying pan, add the aubergine and fry for about 10 minutes until golden. Drain and leave to cool.

2. Mix the herbs, chili, yogurt, and mayonnaise in a bowl and season to taste with salt and pepper.

3. Arrange the fried aubergine slices over the tortillas and spread with the Greek yogurt mixture, then top with the cucumber slices. Roll up each tortilla, sprinkle with paprika and serve.

7.22. Bean & Pepper Burritos

(Serves 4, Cook Time 35-45 Minutes, Difficulty: Normal)

Ingredients:

- 3 red peppers, cored, deseeded and cut into small chunks
- 400 g (13 oz) can black beans, drained
- ½ bunch of spring onions, chopped
- 4 tablespoons chopped fresh coriander
- 1 tablespoon hot pepper sauce
- 100 g (3½ oz) Cheddar cheese, grated
- 4 large tortilla wraps
- salt

Instructions:

1. Heat a frying pan, add the peppers and cook for about 15 minutes, or until softened and lightly browned.

2. Tip the peppers into a bowl and add the beans, spring onions, coriander, and pepper sauce. Mix well. Stir in the cheese and a little salt.

3. Spoon the mixture onto the centers of the tortilla wraps. Spread the filling out into a strip that comes about 3.5 cm (1½ inches) from the edges. Fold these edges over, then roll up each tortilla, start from an unfolded end, to enclose the filling.

4. Wrap each tortilla in heavy-duty foil, then tuck the parcels between hot coals or logs to cook for about 20–30 minutes until cooked through, turning the parcels occasionally, so they cook evenly.

7.23. Sweet Potato, Bacon & Thyme Cakes

(Serves 4, Cook Time 20-30 Minutes, Difficulty: Normal)

Ingredients:

- 250 g (8 oz) sweet potatoes, cut into small chunks
- 1–2 tablespoons vegetable oil
- 125 g (4 oz) streaky bacon, finely diced
- 1 tablespoon chopped thyme
- 1 egg
- 150 ml (¼ pint) buttermilk
- 175 g (6 oz) self-raising flour
- maple syrup or sweet chilly sauce, to serve

Instructions:

1. Cook the sweet potatoes in a saucepan of boiling water for about 5 minutes, or until soft. Drain well, then return to the pan and mash well.

2. Tip into a bowl. Meanwhile, heat 1-tablespoon of the oil in a frying pan, add the diced bacon and fry until crisp. Using a slotted spoon, add to the sweet potatoes, reserving the oil in the pan.

3. Add the thyme, egg, and buttermilk to the sweet potato mixture and beat together to make a smooth batter. Add the flour and stir until evenly mixed.

4. Reheat the frying pan until hot. Scoop a large spoonful of the mixture into the pan, spacing them slightly apart, and cook until golden on the underside, then turn the cakes over and cook on the other side until golden and cooked through. Remove from the pan and serve warm, drizzled with maple syrup or chili sauce.

5. Repeat with the remaining mixture, adding a little more oil to the pan as required.

7.25. Fresh Tomato Sauce

(Serves 4, Cook Time 30 Minutes, Difficulty: Normal)

Ingredients:

- 1 kg (2 lb) very ripe, full-flavoured tomatoes
- 100 ml (3½ Fl oz) olive oil
- 1 onion, finely chopped
- 2 garlic cloves, crushed
- 2 tablespoons chopped oregano
- sprinkling of caster sugar (optional)
- salt and pepper

Instructions:

1. Put the tomatoes in a heatproof bowl, cover with boiling water and leave for about 2 minutes, or until the skins start to split. Pour away the water.

2. Peel and roughly chop the tomatoes. Heat the oil in a large saucepan, add the onion and cook over medium heat for about 5 minutes until softened but not browned. Add the garlic and fry for a further 1 minute.

3. Add the tomatoes and cook for 20–25 minutes, frequently stirring, until the sauce is thickened and pulpy.

4. Stir in the oregano and season to taste with salt and pepper. If the sauce is very sharp, add a sprinkling of caster sugar.

7.26. Chorizo Cherry Tomato Sauce

(Serves 4, Cook Time 25 Minutes, Difficulty: Easy)

Ingredients:

- 3 tablespoons olive oil
- 1 large red onion, finely chopped
- 125 g (4 oz) chorizo sausage, finely diced
- 1 teaspoon fennel or celery seeds
- 400 g (13 oz) can cherry tomatoes
- 1 tablespoon wine vinegar
- 1 tablespoon clear honey
- salt and pepper

Instructions:

1. Heat the oil in a saucepan, add the onion and fry gently, stirring, for about 3 minutes until beginning to soften. Add the chorizo and fennel or celery seeds and fry for a further 2 minutes.

2. Strain the cherry tomatoes through a sieve into the pan, reserving the whole pieces. Add the vinegar, honey and a little salt and pepper to the pan and bring to the boil. Cover with a lid and cook over a low heat for 8minutes.

3. Add the strained tomatoes and adjust the seasoning if necessary. Heat through for 1 minute and serve hot.

7.27. Sauce Vierge

(Serves 6, Cook Time 15 Minutes, Difficulty: Easy)

Ingredients:

- 4 ripe tomatoes
- ½ teaspoon coriander seeds

- large handful of fresh herbs (such as chervil, flat leaf parsley, tarragon and chives)
- 1 garlic clove, finely chopped
- finely grated rind and juice of 1 lemon
- 100 ml (3½ Fl oz) olive oil
- salt and pepper

Instructions:

1. Put the tomatoes in a heatproof bowl, cover with boiling water and leave for about 2 minutes, or until the skins start to split. Pour away the water.

2. Peel the tomatoes, then halve them and scoop out the seeds with a teaspoon.

3. Chop the flesh into small dice.

4. Using a pestle and mortar or the end of a rolling pin, crush the coriander seeds as finely as possible. Discard the stalks from the herbs and finely chop the leaves.

5. Mix the diced tomatoes, coriander seeds, herbs, garlic, lemon rind and juice, and oil with a little salt and pepper in a bowl. Cover with clingfilm and store in a cool box. Heat through over medium heat when ready to serve.

7.28. Lemon & Vodka Sauce

(Serves 2, Cook Time 15 Minutes, Difficulty: Easy)

Ingredients:

- 1 lemon
- 2 tablespoons olive oil
- 2 garlic cloves, thinly sliced
- 1 red chilly, deseeded and thinly sliced
- 2 teaspoons chopped thyme, plus a little extra to garnish
- 100 g (3½ oz) cream cheese

- 2 tablespoons vodka
- salt

Instructions:

1. Pare thin strips of rind from the lemon using a lemon zester or sharp knife. Squeeze 1-tablespoon lemon juice.

2. Heat the oil in a saucepan, add the lemon rind, garlic, chili, and thyme and fry gently for 2–3 minutes, or until the ingredients start to color.

3. Add the cream cheese to the saucepan and heat through until it softens to the consistency of pouring cream. Stir in the vodka, lemon juice, and a little salt and serve hot.

7.29. Dill & Mustard

(Serves 8, Cook Time 10 Minutes, Difficulty: Easy)

Ingredients:

- large handful of dill
- 2 tablespoons mild, wholegrain mustard
- 1 teaspoon Dijon mustard
- 2 tablespoons caster sugar
- 3 tablespoons white wine vinegar
- 150 ml (¼ pint) olive oil
- salt

Instructions:

1. Pull the dill from the sprigs and chop finely. Put the mustards, sugar, and vinegar into a bowl and add a little salt.

2. Whisking constantly, gradually add the oil in a steady stream until the sauce is thick and smooth.

3. Stir in the dill, then taste and adjust the seasoning, adding a little more salt, vinegar or sugar, if liked.

7.30. Sweet Stuff & Drinks Hot Barbecued
(Serves 4, Cook Time 20 Minutes, Difficulty: Easy)

Ingredients:

- Fruit Salad
- 1 small pineapple
- 1 mango
- 1 nectarine, quartered and pitted
- 1 peach, quartered and pitted
- 2 apricots, halved, or quartered if large, and pitted
- 4 tablespoons Greek yogurt
- clear honey, for drizzling
- few cardamom seeds (optional)

Instructions:

1. Top and tail the pineapple and place it on one end on a chopping board.

2. Using a sharp knife, cut downwards to remove the skin, working all around the pineapple. Cut the pineapple flesh into chunks – in a small pineapple the core is usually sweet and soft enough to eat.

3. Peel the mango and cut it into slices on either side of the stone. Cook the mango and pineapple on a grill rack over a hot barbecue or campfire for 4 minutes on each side and the nectarine, peach and apricots for 3 minutes on each side, until lightly charred. If you like, thread the fruit pieces on to metal skewers before cooking.

4. Serve the griddled fruit topped with Greek yogurt, drizzled with clear honey and scattered with cardamom seeds, if using.

7.31. Fruit Salad Kebabs

(Serves 4, Cook Time 35 Minutes, Difficulty: Normal)

Ingredients:

- ½ large pineapple
- 1 papaya
- 1 peach, halved and pitted
- 8 large strawberries, hulled
- Greek yogurt, to serve
- Syrup
- ¼ teaspoon Chinese 5-spice powder
- 100 g (3½ oz) light brown sugar
- grated rind and juice of 1 lemon

Instructions:

1. Put all the syrup ingredients and 125 ml (4 Fl oz) water in a small saucepan and bring slowly to the boil, occasionally stirring, until the sugar has dissolved, then boil rapidly for 1 minute. Leave to cool slightly.

2. Cut the green top off the pineapple, then cut away the skin. Cut into 8-wedges, cutting through the top down to the base. Remove the core, then thickly slice the wedges. Put the fruit into a shallow dish.

3. Quarter the papaya and scoop out the black seeds with a spoon. Peel away the skin, then thickly slice. Cut the peach into chunks and halve the strawberries. Mix all the fruit in a bowl and pour the warm syrup over. Cover with clingfilm and leave to infuse for 1 hour, or overnight, if preferred.

4. Thread the fruit on to 8 metal skewers (or wooden skewers that have been soaked in cold water for 30 minutes) and cook on a grill rack over a hot barbecue or campfire for about 10 minutes, turning several times and brushing with the syrup, until hot and browned around the edges.

5. Serve the kebabs with a spoonful of yogurt mixed with a little of the syrup, if liked.

7.32. Griddled Peaches with Passion Fruit

(Serves 4, Cook Time 15 Minutes, Difficulty: Easy)

Ingredients:

- 6 large ripe peaches, halved and pitted
- 2 tablespoons clear honey, plus extra
- to serve 2 teaspoons ground cinnamon

To serve:

- 125 g (4 oz) Greek yogurt pulp from 2 passion fruit

Instructions:

1. Cook the peach halves, cut side down, on a grill rack over a hot barbecue or campfire for about 3–4 minutes, or until lightly charred. Turn the peaches over, drizzle with the honey and dust with cinnamon, then cook for a further 2 minutes, or until softened.

2. Transfer to bowls and serve topped with Greek yogurt and the passion fruit pulp.

7.33. Creole Pineapple Wedges

(Serves 4-6, Cook Time 20 Minutes, Difficulty: Easy)

Ingredients:

- 1 small pineapple, about 1.25 kg (2½ lb)
- 1 tablespoon dark rum

- juice of 1 lime
- 15 g (½ oz) sesame seeds

Instructions:

1. Cut the pineapple lengthways, first in half and then into quarters, leaving the leaves intact. The wedges should be about 1 cm (½ inch) thick, so it may be necessary to divide the quarters again.

2. Mix the dark rum and lime juice in a bowl, then sprinkle the mixture over the pineapple slices.

3. Cook the pineapple on a grill rack over a hot barbecue or campfire for about 10 minutes, turning to ensure even cooking. Serve sprinkled with sesame seeds.

7.34. Mini Strawberry Shortcakes

(Serves 4, Cook Time 20 Minutes, Difficulty: Easy)

Ingredients:

- 250 g (8 oz) cream cheese
- 2 teaspoons icing sugar
- 8 digestive biscuits or homemade biscuits
- 4 teaspoons strawberry jam
- 250 g (8 oz) strawberries, hulled and sliced

Instructions:

1. Beat the cream cheese in a bowl to soften, then stir in the icing sugar. Spread a biscuit with 1-teaspoon of the strawberry jam, then spread a quarter of the cream cheese mixture over the biscuit. Lay a few strawberry slices on top of the cream cheese, then top with a second biscuit.

2. Repeat to make 3-more shortcakes. Transfer to a plastic box with a lid and chill in a cool box for a least 1 hour before serving.

7.35. Tipsy Blueberry Pots & Mascarpone

(Serves 4, Cook Time 25 Minutes, Difficulty: Normal)

Ingredients:

- 200 g (7 oz) blueberries
- 2 tablespoons kirsch or vodka
- 150 g (5 oz) mascarpone cheese
- 150 g (5 oz) natural yogurt
- 2 tablespoons caster sugar
- grated rind and juice of 1 lime

Instructions:

1. Mix three-quarters of the blueberries and the alcohol in a bowl, cover with clingfilm, and leave to soak for at least 1 hour. Mash the blueberries.

2. Beat together the mascarpone and yogurt in a separate bowl until smooth, then mix in the sugar and lime rind and juice.

3. Layer alternate spoonful of mashed blueberries and mascarpone in owls or glasses, top with the whole blueberries, and serve.

7.36. Sweet & Sour Spiced

(Serves 4, Cook Time 18 Minutes, Difficulty: Easy)

Ingredients:

- Pineapple & Mango
- 1 firm, ripe mango
- 1 small pineapple, sliced in half lengthways and then into thin wedges
- 2 tablespoons icing sugar, plus extra to serve
- Sweet and sour dressing

- ½ long red chilly, deseeded and finely chopped
- 4 tablespoons lime juice
- 2 tablespoons soft light brown sugar
- 1–2 tablespoons finely shredded mint

Instructions:

1. Heat a griddle pan over medium-high heat. Cut the mango into 2-pieces, using the stone as a guide and cutting either side of it. Sift icing sugar all over the mango and pineapple's cut sides, so they are well covered. Lay the mango, cut side down, and pineapple in the hot pan and griddle for 2 minutes, twisting the pieces once so that a charred criss-cross pattern appears on the fruit. Turn the pineapple wedges over and repeat on the other side. It may need to be done in two batches.

2. Meanwhile, to make the sweet and sour dressing, put the chili, lime juice, sugar, and mint in a small bowl, then stir until the sugar is dissolved. Set aside.

3. Transfer the fruits to plates and drizzle over the dressing. Serve dusted with extra icing sugar, if liked.

7.37. Passion Fruit Yogurt Fool

(Serves 4, Cook Time 10 Minutes, Difficulty: Easy)

Ingredients:

- 200 ml (7 Fl oz) whipping cream
- 6 passion fruit, halved, flesh and seeds removed
- 300 ml (½ pint) Greek yogurt
- 1 tablespoon clear honey
- 4 pieces of shortbread or homemade biscuits, to serve

Instructions:

1. Whip the cream in a bowl until it forms soft peaks.

2. Put the passion fruit flesh and seeds, yogurt, and honey in a separate bowl and stir together, then fold in the cream.

3. Spoon into tall glasses or bowls and serve with the biscuits.

7.38. Figs with Yogurt & Honey

(Serves 4-6, Cook Time 15 Minutes, Difficulty: Easy)

Instructions:

- 8 ripe figs
- 4 tablespoons natural yogurt
- 2 tablespoons clear honey

Instructions:

1. Heat a griddle pan until hot. Slice the figs in half, then add to the pan, skin side down, and cook for 10 minutes until the skins begin to blacken.

2. Serve the figs with spoonfuls of yogurt, and some honey spooned over the top.

7.39. Lemon & Passion Fruit Whips

(Serves 2, Cook Time 15 Minutes, Difficulty: Easy)

Instruction:

- 50 g (2 oz) shortbread biscuits, crushed
- 150 ml (¼ pint) double cream
- 120 g (4 oz) pot lemon yogurt
- 2 passion fruit, halved

Instructions:

1. Divide the crushed biscuits between two glasses or bowls. Whip the cream in a bowl until just thick enough to form soft peaks, then lightly fold in the yogurt with the seeds and pulp from 1 of the passion fruits.

2. Spoon the mixture into the glasses, spoon the remaining passion fruit seeds and pulp over the top and serve.

7.40. Stewed Rhubarb with Custard

(Serves 4-6, Cook Time 25 Minutes, Difficulty: Easy)

Ingredients:

- 750 g (1½ lb) rhubarb, cut into 3.5 cm (1½ inch) lengths
- 3 tablespoons orange juice or water
- ½ teaspoon ground ginger (optional)
- 50–100 g (2–3½ oz) caster sugar
- 600 ml (1 pint) ready-made custard

Instructions:

1. Put the rhubarb, orange juice, or water and ground ginger if used in a large saucepan. Add as much of the remaining sugar as you like, depending on the sweetness desired, to the rhubarb. Heat until the sugar has dissolved, then simmer gently, occasionally stirring,

for about 8 minutes, or until the rhubarb is tender. Remove from the heat and leave to cool slightly.

2. Heat the custard in a separate saucepan according to the packet instructions.

3. Spoon the rhubarb into bowls and serve with the custard

7.41. Blueberry & Orange Eton Mess

(Serves 4-6, Cook Time 15 Minutes, Difficulty: Easy)

Ingredients:

- 250 ml (8 fl oz) fresh vanilla custard
- 200 g (7 oz) blueberry yogurt
- 1 teaspoon finely grated orange rind

- 1 teaspoon vanilla bean paste or extract
- 150 g (5 oz) blueberries
- 4 ready-made meringues nests

Instructions:

1. Put the custard, yogurt, orange rind and vanilla bean paste or extract in a bowl and stir until well combined.

2. Put two-thirds of the blueberries in four glasses or bowls. Spoon over the blueberry yogurt mixture, then top each glass with a lightly crushed meringue. Sprinkle over the remaining blueberries and serve immediately

7.42. Cinnamon & Raisin Pear Trifle

(Serves 4, Cook Time 20-30 Minutes, Difficulty: Easy)

Ingredients:

- 75 g (3 oz) raisins
- 1 teaspoon cinnamon
- 400 g (13 oz) can pears in juice
- 500 g (1 lb) fresh vanilla custard
- 175 g (6 oz) panettone, cut into bite-sized cubes
- 4 tablespoons crème fraîche
- 50 g (2 oz) roasted hazelnuts, roughly chopped

Instructions:

1. Put the raisins, half of the cinnamon, and 100 ml (3½ Fl oz) of the juice from the pears in a saucepan over medium-high heat and bring up to a gentle boil, then simmer over low heat for 1 minute. Turn off the heat and leave to stand for 5 minutes.

2. Beat the custard with the remaining cinnamon in a bowl and slice the pears into thick pieces.

3. Place the panettone in the bottom of four bowls. Pour the warm raisin mixture over the panettone cubes and cover with the sliced pears. Pour over the custard, cover with clingfilm, and chill in a cool box for about 10 minutes.

4. Spoon one tablespoon of the crème fraîche over each trifle and serve scattered with the hazelnuts.

7.43. Chocolate & Banana Melts

(Serves 4, Cook Time 10 Minutes, Difficulty: Easy)

Ingredients:

- 8 slices of white bread, crusts removed
- 75 g (3 oz) dark chocolate, finely chopped
- 1 large banana, sliced
- 50 g (2 oz) marshmallows, chopped
- vegetable oil, for brushing

Instructions:

1. Place half the bread slices on a board and top each with the chocolate, banana, and marshmallows. Top with the remaining bread. Brush the sandwiches lightly with oil and cook on a grill rack over a barbecue or campfire for 1–2 minutes.

2. Flip the sandwiches over and cook for a further 1–2 minutes until golden.

7.44. Blueberry & Ginger Patties

(Serves 4, Cook Time 30-40 Minutes, Difficulty: Normal)

Ingredients:

- 200 g (7 oz) self-raising flour, plus extra for dusting
- 1 teaspoon baking powder

- 50 g (2 oz) slightly salted butter, cubed
- 2 pieces of stem ginger, finely chopped
- 75 g (3 oz) dried blueberries
- 25 g (1 oz) caster sugar, plus extra for dusting
- 75 ml (3 Fl oz) milk
- vegetable oil, for frying
- clotted cream or Greek yogurt, to serve

Instructions:

1. Put the flour and baking powder in a bowl, add the butter and rub in with the fingertips until the mixture resembles fine breadcrumbs. Stir in the ginger, blueberries, and sugar.

2. Add the milk to the bowl and mix with a round-bladed knife to make a soft dough. Turn out onto a lightly floured board and shape into a log.

3. Cut across into 12 pieces, all roughly the same size and about 1 cm (½ inch) thick.

4. Heat a little oil in a frying pan, add several of the patties and cook until golden on the underside. Turn the patties over and cook for a further few minutes until golden and cooked through. Remove from the pan, lightly dust with sugar, and serve warm with clotted cream or yogurt.

5. Repeat with the remaining patties, adding a little more oil to the pan as required.

7.45. S'mores

(Serves 18, Cook Time 25 Minutes, Difficulty: Normal)

Ingredients:

- 200 g (7 oz) milk chocolate, broken into pieces
- 18 marshmallows
- plenty of bought or homemade sweet biscuits

Instructions:

1. Put the chocolate in a heatproof bowl and place it on a grill rack over the coolest area of a barbecue or campfire.

2. Thread the marshmallows on to several metal skewers, leaving a space between each, then head over the fire, turning them until lightly toasted.

3. For each 's'more,' spread a little melted chocolate onto a biscuit, top with a toasted marshmallow, and then another chocolate-coated biscuit, pressing the biscuits together gently, so the marshmallow spreads to form a filling.

7.46. Choc Cinnamon

(Serves 2, Cook Time 10 Minutes, Difficulty: Easy)

Ingredients:

- Eggy Bread
- 2 eggs
- 2 thick slices of seeded brown bread, cut in half
- 1 tablespoon butter
- 2 tablespoons caster sugar
- 2 teaspoons cocoa powder
- ½ teaspoon ground cinnamon

Instruction:

1. Lightly beat the eggs in a shallow dish. Dip the bread slices in the mixture, turning them over so they've absorbed the batter on both sides.

2. Melt the butter in a frying pan until foaming, add the eggy bread and cook for about 5 minutes, occasionally turning, until golden on both sides.

3. Mix the sugar, cocoa powder, and cinnamon on a plate. Transfer the hot eggy bread to the plate and coat in the mixture. Serve immediately.

7.47. Quick Kiwifruit & Ginger Cheesecakes

(Serves 4, Cook Time 10-20 Minutes, Difficulty: Easy)

Ingredients:

- 75 g (3 oz) gingernut biscuits
- 100 g (3½ oz) cream cheese
- 75 g (3 oz) crème fraîche
- 1 piece of stem ginger, about 15 g (½ oz), chopped 1 tablespoon stem
- ginger syrup
- 2 kiwi-fruit, peeled and sliced

Instructions:

1. Put the gingernut biscuits in a plastic bag and crush them using a rolling pin.

2. Sprinkle the crushed biscuits over the bottom of four glasses or bowls. Beat the cream cheese, crème fraîche, stem ginger, and syrup in a bowl, then spoon the mixture over the biscuits. Arrange the kiwifruit on top of the cheesecakes and serve.

7.48. Glossy Chocolate Sauce

(Serves 4-6, Cook Time 15-20 Minutes, Difficulty: Easy)

Ingredients:

- 125 g (4 oz) caster sugar
- 200 g (7 oz) plain dark chocolate, chopped
- 2 tablespoons unsalted butter

Instructions:

1. Put the sugar and 125 ml (4 Fl oz) water in a small saucepan and cook over low heat, constantly stirring with a wooden spoon, until the sugar has completely dissolved.

2. Bring the syrup to the boil and boil for 1 minute, then remove the pan from the heat and leave to cool for 1 minute. Tip the chocolate into the pan.

3. Add the butter and leave until the chocolate and butter have melted, frequently stirring until the sauce is smooth and glossy. If the last of the chocolate doesn't melt completely or you want to serve the sauce warm, return the pan briefly to very low heat.

7.49. Apple Sauce

(Serves 6, Cook Time 30 Minutes, Difficulty: Normal)

Ingredients:

- 4 tablespoons butter
- 3 large cooking apples, peeled, cored and chopped
- 50 g (2 oz) caster sugar
- 6 whole cloves
- finely grated rind and juice of 1 lemon
- salt

Instructions:

1. Melt the butter in a saucepan and add the apples, sugar, cloves, lemon rind and juice, and a little salt. Cover with a lid and leave to cook gently over the lowest heat for about 20 minutes, stirring the mixture occasionally, until the apples are very soft and mushy.

2. Adjust the seasoning if necessary, adding a little more lemon juice for a tangier flavor, if liked. Transfer to a bowl and serve warm or cold.

7.50. Mulled Cranberry & Red Wine

(Serves 8-10, Cook Time 25 Minutes, Difficulty: Easy)

Ingredients:

- 750 ml (1¼ pint) bottle inexpensive red wine
- 600 ml (1 pint) cranberry juice
- 100 ml (3½ Fl oz) brandy, rum, vodka or orange liqueur

- 100 g (3½ oz) caster sugar
- 1 orange
- 8 cloves
- 1–2 cinnamon sticks (depending on size)

To serve:

- 1 orange, cut into segments
- 2–3 bay leaves
- few fresh cranberries

Instructions:

1. Pour the red wine, cranberry juice, brandy, or other alcohol into a large saucepan and stir in the sugar.

2. Stud the orange segments with a clove. Break the cinnamon sticks into large pieces and add to the pan with the orange pieces. Cover with a lid and heat gently for about 10 minutes until warm.

3. Replace the orange segments with fresh ones and add the bay leaves and cranberries.

Ladle into heatproof glasses or mugs, keeping back the fruits and herbs, if liked.

7.51. Frothy Hot Toddy Chocolate Drink
(Serves 1, Cook Time 15 Minutes, Difficulty: Easy)

Ingredients:

- 1 teaspoon cornflour
- 300 ml (½ pint) semi-skimmed milk
- 1 teaspoon golden granulated sugar
- 4 squares of plain dark chocolate
- 2 tablespoons alcohol of your choice (such as brandy, rum or vodka)

- 1 teaspoon chocolate (plain dark, milk or white), grated, to serve

Instructions:

1. Put the cornflour in a jug and mix in 1 tablespoon of the milk to smooth paste. Stir in 200 ml (7 Fl oz) of the milk, sugar, chocolate, and alcohol.

2. Pour into a saucepan and heat through until hot, then pour into a tall mug.

3. Heat the remaining milk and whisk vigorously. Pour over the hot chocolate, sprinkle over the grated chocolate and serve immediately.

7.52. Rusty Nail

(Serves 1, Cook Time 10-20 Minutes, Difficulty: Easy)

Ingredients:

- ice cubes, if available
- 1½ measures Scotch whisky
- 1 measure
- Drambuie

Instructions:

1. Fill a short glass with ice cubes, if using. Pour over the whisky and Drambuie and serve.

7.53. Whisky MAC

(Serves 2, Cook Time 15 Minutes, Difficulty: Easy)

Ingredients:

- 3–4 ice cubes, if available
- 1 measure Scotch whisky
- 1 measure ginger wine

Instructions:

1. Put the ice cubes, if using, in a short glass. Pour over the whisky and ginger wine, stir lightly and serve.

7.54. Pimm's Cocktail

(Serves 1, Cook Time 10 Minutes, Difficulty: Easy)

Ingredients:

- ice cubes, if available
- 1 measure Pimm's No. 1
- cucumber slices
- 1 strawberry
- apple slices
- lemon slices
- orange slices
- 3 measures lemonade
- 1 mint sprig, to garnish

Instructions:

1. Fill a tall glass with ice, if using, then add the Pimm's.

2. Put the cucumber and fruit slices in the glass and top up with the lemonade. Decorate with the mint sprig and serve.

7.55. Beer Flatbreads with Cheese & Onions

(Serves 6, Cook Time 55 Minutes, Difficulty: Normal)

Ingredients:

- 300 g (10 oz) strong white bread flour, plus extra for dusting

- 1 teaspoon salt
- 1 teaspoon fast-action dried yeast
- 4 tablespoons olive oil
- 2 teaspoons Dijon mustard
- 150 ml (¼ pint) strong ale
- 2 medium onions, chopped
- 100 g (3½ oz) Cheddar or Gruyère cheese, grated

Instructions:

1. Put the flour, salt, yeast, 3-tablespoons of the oil, and the mustard in a bowl and stir in the ale. Mix with a round-bladed knife to make a soft dough, adding a little more ale or water if it is dry. Tip out onto a lightly floured board and knead for about 10 minutes until the dough is smooth and elastic. (If you've no surface to work on, work the dough in the bowl as best as you can.) Return the dough to the bowl, cover with a tea towel or clingfilm and leave in a warm place (near the fire if already lit) until the dough has doubled in size.

2. Meanwhile, heat the remaining oil in a frying pan, add the onions and cook over low heat for about 15 minutes, frequently stirring, until soft and deep golden. Leave to cool.

3. Divide the dough into 12 pieces and roll out each on a floured board to around about 16 cm (6½ inches) in diameter. Sprinkle the centers of 6 of the rounds with cheese and spoon the onions on top. Brush the edges lightly with water and press another round of dough on top, so the filling is sandwiched. Flatten out with a rolling pin until the dough is so thin that the filling shows through.

4. Heat a large dry frying pan or griddle pan, add 1-bread and cook until pale golden on the underside. Flip the bread over and cook on the other side until the dough is cooked through, about 5–7 minutes in total. Wrap in foil and keep warm. Repeat with the remaining bread.

7.56. Corn Flatbreads with Sweetcorn & Gruyère

(Serves 4, Cook Time 40 Minutes, Difficulty: Normal)

Ingredients:

- 100 g (3½ oz) masa harina flour
- 100 g (3½ oz) self-raising flour, plus extra for dusting
- 1 teaspoon salt
- 2 tablespoons olive oil

Topping:

- 150 g (5 oz) Gruyère cheese, grated
- 125 g (4 oz) canned sweetcorn, drained
- 4 tomatoes, thinly sliced
- 1 Little Gem lettuce, shredded
- sweet chilly sauce
- soured cream

Instructions:

1. Put the flours, salt, and olive oil in a bowl and stir in 150 ml (¼ pint) cold water to make a soft dough. Divide the dough into 4-even-sized pieces and roll out each as thinly as possible on a well-floured board to rounds about 20 cm (8 inches) in diameter.

2. Heat a dry frying pan for 5 minutes, add 1-flatbread and cook for about 2–4 minutes on each side until pale golden and cooked through. Slide-out of the pan onto a sheet of foil and keep warm. Repeat with the remaining flatbreads.

3. To heat through and serve, sprinkle a thin layer of cheese and sweet pop over a flatbread and add several tomato slices. Return to the stove or fire, either in the pan or on a sheet of foil, and heat through until the cheese starts to melt.

4. Scatter with shredded lettuce, drizzle with chili sauce, and a little soured cream and fold or roll up to serve.

5. Repeat with the remaining flatbreads and toppings.

7.57. Balsamic Braised Leeks & Peppers

(Serves 4, Cook Time 20 Minutes, Difficulty: Easy)

Ingredients:

- 2 tablespoons olive oil
- 2 leeks, trimmed and cut into 1 cm (½ inch) pieces
- 1 orange pepper, cored, deseeded and cut into 1 cm (½ inch) chunks
- 1 red pepper, cored, deseeded and cut into 1 cm (½ inch) chunks
- 3 tablespoons balsamic vinegar handful of flat leaf parsley, chopped salt and pepper

Instructions:

1. Heat the oil in a saucepan, add the leeks and peppers and stir well. Cover with a lid and cook very gently for 10 minutes.

2. Add the balsamic vinegar and cook, uncovered, for a further 10 minutes. The vegetables should be brown from the vinegar, and all the liquid should have evaporated.

3. Season well with salt and pepper, then stir in the chopped parsley just before serving.

7.58. Mustard & Thyme Sweet Potatoes

(Serves 6, Cook Time 40 Minutes, Difficulty: Normal)

Ingredients:

- 6 sweet potatoes, about 250 g (8 oz) each, scrubbed
- Mustard and thyme butter
- 125 g (4 oz) butter, softened
- 1 tablespoon wholegrain mustard
- 1 teaspoon chopped thyme

- pepper

Instructions:

1. Wrap each potato in a double layer of foil, then tuck between hot coals or logs, allowing some of the coals or logs to cover the potatoes—Cook for about 40 minutes, or until tender, rotating the parcels several times during cooking.

2. Meanwhile, to make the mustard and thyme butter, put the butter, mustard, thyme, and some pepper in a bowl and mash with a fork until evenly mixed. Set aside.

3. Carefully remove the potatoes from the foil parcels. Cut in half and serve topped with the butter.

7.59. Fire-Baked New Potatoes with Green Dressing

(Serves 6, Cook Time 30 Minutes, Difficulty: Hard)

Ingredients:

- 500 g (1 lb) new potatoes, scrubbed and rinsed
- 100 ml (3½ Fl oz) olive oil
- large handful each of parsley and chives, chopped
- 2 tablespoons chopped mint
- 2 tablespoons capers, drained and chopped
- 1 tablespoon lemon juice
- 2 teaspoons clear honey
- salt and pepper

Instructions:

1. Put the potatoes on a large square of heavy-duty foil. Drizzle with 1-tablespoon of the oil and season with salt and pepper. Bring the foil up around the potatoes and seal well, then tuck the parcel between hot coals or logs to cook. It will take 1–2 hours, depending on the intensity of the fire.

2. Rotate the parcel several times during cooking, so the potatoes cook evenly.

3. Mix the herbs, capers, remaining oil, lemon juice, honey, and a little salt and pepper in a small bowl.

4. Carefully unwrap the foil and spoon the dressing over the potatoes to serve.

7.60. Balsamic-Roasted Tomatoes

(Serves 6, Cook Time 40 Minutes, Difficulty: Normal)

Ingredients:

- 12 plum tomatoes, halved
- 2 tablespoons olive oil
- 2 teaspoons balsamic vinegar
- 1 small bunch of basil
- 2 tablespoons pine nuts
- 4 slices of ciabatta bread
- salt and pepper

Instructions:

1. Put the tomatoes, cut side up, on a large piece of heavy-duty foil, and drizzle with the oil and vinegar. Tear half the basil over the top, add the pine nuts, and season with salt and pepper.

2. Bring the foil up around the tomatoes and seal well, then tuck between hot coals or logs to cook for about 30–40 minutes, or until softened.

3. Rotate the parcel several times during cooking.

4. Toast the bread, cut side down, on a rack over the barbecue or campfire, until charred.

5. Carefully unwrap the foil and spoon the tomatoes on to the toast.

6. Sprinkle with the remaining basil leaves and serve immediately.

7.61. Roasted Red Onions

(Serves 4, Cook Time 1 Hour, Difficulty: Normal)

Ingredients:

- handful each of bay leaves and thyme
- 8 small red onions, peeled
- 2 tablespoons olive oil
- 3 tablespoons balsamic glaze
- salt and pepper

Instructions:

1. Scatter the herbs onto a large piece of heavy-duty foil and put the onions on top. Drizzle with the oil and season lightly with salt and pepper.

2. Bring the foil up around the onions and seal well, then tuck between hot coals or logs to cook for about 40–50 minutes, or until softened. Carefully unwrap the foil and drizzle the onions with the balsamic glaze.

3. Re-seal the parcel and return to the fire until the onions are soft.

7.62. Panzanella Originating from Tuscany, Italy

(Serves 4, Cook Time 15 Minutes, Difficulty: Easy)

Ingredients:

- 4 slices of ciabatta bread
- 4 ripe tomatoes, cored and chopped
- ½ cucumber, deseeded, peeled and cubed
- 1 red onion, chopped
- handful of chopped flat leaf parsley
- 1 tablespoon chopped pitted black olives

- 50 ml (2 Fl oz) olive oil
- 1–2 tablespoons wine vinegar
- juice of ½ lemon
- salt and pepper

Instructions:

1. Toast the bread lightly in a griddle pan or on a rack over a barbecue or campfire, tear it into pieces, and put it in a large bowl. Add the tomatoes, cucumber, onion, parsley, and olives.

2. Mix the oil, vinegar, and lemon juice in a bowl and season with salt and pepper.

3. Pour the dressing over the salad and mix well. Cover and leave to stand for at least 1 hour to allow the flavors to mingle.

7.63. Crushed Minted Peas

(Serves 4-6, Cook Time 20 Minutes, Difficulty: Normal)

Ingredients:

- 400 g (13 oz) fresh peas, shelled
- several sprigs of mint
- 2 tablespoons butter
- 2 tablespoons crème fraîche
- salt and pepper

Instructions:

1. Cook the peas with the mint in a large saucepan of boiling water for about 5 minutes, or until very tender. Drain and return to the pan, discarding the mint.

2. Stir in the butter and crème fraîche and use a fork to crush the peas roughly—season to taste with salt and pepper and reheat gently.

Chapter 8: Camping Vegetarian Main and Side Recipes

In this chapter, we will provide you amazing and healthy Vegetarian Recipes that you can cook while camping.

8.1. Easy Skillet Mexican Corn on the Cob

(Serves 4-6, Cook Time 10 Minutes, Difficulty: Normal)

Ingredients:

- 6 Ears of Fresh Corn, (Husks Removed and Kernels Cut off Cob)
- 1 Tbsp. Butter
- 1/2 Cup of Reduced Fat Mayo
- 1 Tbsp. Chili Powder
- Juice from 1 Lime
- 2 Tsp. Kosher Salt
- 1 Tsp. Cracked Black Pepper
- 1/4 Cup Chopped Cilantro
- 1/2 Cup Cojita cheese

Instructions:

1. Combine mayo, chili powder, lime juice, 1 Tsp. 1/2 Tsp. of salt and Pepper until everything's mixed. Only put aside. Over the medium-high fire, heat a cast-iron skillet.

Add butter to the pan and allow it to begin to melt. Add the corn kernels and the remaining salt and Pepper to your skillet and spread out evenly. Until stirring, let the corn blister for a few minutes.

2. When you begin to hear the corn popping its moment to stir, a strong tip is.

Repeat this step for around 5-7 minutes until the corn is mildly burned, but not burnt. Minimize heat to low and stir in the mixture of chili mayo.

3. Turn off heat, crumble cojita cheese on top and sprinkle with cilantro.

8.2. African Sweet Potato and Peanut Stew

(Serves 4, Cook Time 35 Minutes, Difficulty: Normal)

Ingredients:

- 1 tablespoon oil
- 1 small onion, diced (to yield 1 1/2 cups)
- 2 cloves garlic, minced (about 1 tablespoon)
- 1 medium sweet potato, chopped into 1/4-inch cubes (to yield 2 cups)
- 2 cups broth
- 14 oz. can diced tomatoes
- 1/4 cup peanut butter
- 2 teaspoons New Mexico chili powder
- 1 teaspoon salt
- 14 oz. can chickpeas, drained
- 2 cups Tuscan kale

Instructions:

1. Heat the oil over medium heat in a Dutch oven. Add the onion and sauté for about 5 minutes, until the onion is transparent and brown in patches.

2. Add the garlic and sauté for about 1 minute until it is fragrant. Add the sweet potato, broth, tomatoes & their juices, chili powder, peanut butter, and salt. To guarantee that the peanut butter is fully mixed in, whisk well, and there are no clumps left. Simmer, exposed, or until the sweet potatoes are tender, for around 15-20 minutes.

3. Add the chickpeas and the kale to the Dutch oven until the sweet potatoes are tender. Till the chickpeas have warmed through and the kale has wilted, swirl to mix and heat.

8.3. Tuscan White Bean Skillet with Tomatoes, Mushroom, and Arti Chokes
(Serves 4, Cook Time 35 Minutes, Difficulty: Normal)

Ingredients:

- 2 tablespoons extra virgin olive oil, divided
- 8 ounces brown mushrooms, sliced
- 1 1/2 cups diced yellow onion (about 1 large onion)
- 3 cloves garlic, minced
- 2/3 cup drained and chopped oil-packed sun-dried tomatoes
- 2 14.5-ounce cans fire-roasted diced tomatoes
- 2 14.5-ounce cans drained and rinsed Cannelini beans
- 14.5-ounce can quartered artichoke hearts, rinsed
- 1/2 teaspoon kosher salt
- 1/2 teaspoon black pepper
- 1 teaspoon dried oregano
- 1/2 teaspoon dried thyme
- 1 teaspoon sugar

- Parsley for garnish

Instructions:

1. In a 10-inch or 12-inch cast-iron skillet set over medium-high heat, heat one tablespoon of the oil until it shimmers.

2. Function in batches, in a single sheet, apply the mushrooms to the pan. Brown on either side for 1 to 2 minutes; add to a bowl and repeat for the remaining mushrooms.

3. Apply the remaining tablespoon of oil to the pan; add the onions and sauté for about 3 minutes, until lightly browned.

4. Attach the garlic and sun-dried tomatoes and roast for a further 2 minutes, until fragrant and softened. With the beans, artichoke hearts, salt, Pepper, oregano, thyme, and honey, add the pan's diced tomatoes.

5. Cover the pan and dial down the heat to a low amount. Let it cook for 10 minutes or so until hot. Place the mushrooms back in the pan and cook for an extra minute or two to steam them up.

6. Add sliced parsley to the garnish and serve with plenty of crusty bread.

8.4 Skillet Veggie Lasagna

(Serves 4, Cook Time 40 Minutes, Difficulty: Normal)

Ingredients:

- 1 tablespoon olive oil
- 1 small white onion, diced
- 1 small carrot, peeled and diced
- 1 small red bell pepper, cored and diced
- 1 small zucchini, diced
- 4 garlic cloves, minced
- Kosher salt and black pepper

- 8 whole uncooked lasagna noodles, each broken into 3–4 pieces
- 1 (24-ounce) jar good-quality pasta sauce
- 1 (15-ounce) can crushed tomatoes
- 1/4 teaspoon crushed red pepper flakes
- 1/2 cup ricotta cheese
- 4 ounces mozzarella ball, torn into pieces (or 1/2 cup shredded mozzarella)

Toppings:

- Shredded fresh basil leaves, grated parmesan, extra crushed red peppers

Instructions:

1. In a 10-inch or 12-inch cast-iron skillet set over medium-high heat, heat one tablespoon of the oil until it shimmers.

2. Function in batches, in a single sheet, apply the mushrooms to the pan. Brown on either side for 1 to 2 minutes; add to a bowl and repeat for the remaining mushrooms.

3. Apply the remaining tablespoon of oil to the pan; add the onions and sauté for about 3 minutes, until lightly browned.

4. Attach the garlic and sun-dried tomatoes and roast for a further 2 minutes, until fragrant and softened. With the beans, artichoke hearts, salt, Pepper, oregano, thyme, and honey, add the pan's diced tomatoes.

5. Cover the pan and dial down the heat to a low amount. Let it cook for 10 minutes or so until hot. Place the mushrooms back in the pan and cook for an extra minute or two to steam them up.

6. Add sliced parsley to the garnish and serve with plenty of crusty bread.

8.5 Easy Migas Recipe

(Serves 4, Cook Time 15 Minutes, Difficulty: Normal)

Ingredients:

- 3 tablespoons olive oil
- 6 large eggs
- 1/2 teaspoon coarse kosher salt
- 8 corn tortillas, cut into eighths

Toppings:

- Chopped cilantro, diced tomatoes, queso fresco.

Instructions:

1. Heat olive oil over medium to high heat in a large nonstick skillet. When the oil is heating up, in a medium dish, whisk the eggs and set them aside.

2. In the pan, add the corn tortillas and fry until crispy, around 6 to 8 minutes.

3. Place the whisked eggs and salt together and fold into the crispy tortillas. Cook until the eggs are fully cooked and no longer runny, for around 2 to 4 minutes.

4. Remove from the sun, sample, and season to taste with more salt. If needed, serve with chopped cilantro, sliced tomatoes, and queso fresco.

8.6. Garlic Parmesan Broccoli and Potatoes in Foil

(Serves 4, Cook Time 15 Minutes, Difficulty: Normal)

Ingredients:

- 3 tablespoons olive oil
- 3 cloves garlic, minced
- 1 tablespoon Italian seasoning

- 1/4 teaspoon onion powder Kosher salt and freshly ground black pepper, to taste
- 24 ounces broccoli florets*
- 16 ounces baby potatoes, halved
- 1/4 cup freshly grated Parmesan
- 2 tablespoons chopped fresh parsley leaves

Instructions:

1. Preheat the oven to 400 ° F. Mix the olive oil, garlic, Italian seasoning, and onion powder in a small bowl; season with salt and pepper to taste.

2. Break four sheets of foil that are nearly 12 inches long. Divide the broccoli and potatoes into four equal parts, and apply a single sheet to each foil's middle.

3. Fold all 4 sides of each packet of foil up. Spoon over the broccoli and potatoes with the garlic mixture. Fold the sides of the foil over the vegetables, cover and seal the closed packages completely.

4. On a baking sheet, put foil packets in a single layer. Place in the oven and bake for 15-25 minutes, until tender.

5. Serve promptly and, if desired, sprinkle with parmesan and parsley.

8.7. Middle Eastern Spiced Camp Fire Chickpeas
(Serves 2, Cook Time 30 Minutes, Difficulty: Normal)

Ingredients:

- 2 tbsp. whole cumin seeds
- 1 tbsp. whole coriander seeds
- 2 tbsp. freshly ground black pepper
- 1 tbsp. smoked mild paprika
- 1 tbsp. whole cloves
- 1 tsp. freshly grated nutmeg

- 1 tsp. ground cinnamon
- 1 tbsp. whole allspice berries

For the Spiced Chickpeas:

- 4 tbsp. sunflower oil
- 1 large onion
- 1 tbsp. 7 spice mix
- 1 400gram tin chickpeas in water
- 100 grams seasonal greens spinach, chard, kale, spicy Chinese greens, etc.
- Sea salt to taste

Instructions:

1. In a small, dry pan, put the cumin and coriander seeds over medium heat and toast before the cumin seeds begin to pop. Shift to a large mortar and pestle the toasted seeds together with the remaining ingredients and grind to a powder to find.

2. Transfer to an air-tight jar and place for up to 12 months in a dark cupboard.

Get a strong fire going and heat the sunflower oil in your cooking pan to prepare the spiced chickpeas. I've got a fondness for cast iron, so there's going to be a camping cooking pot or even a Dutch oven suspended on a tripod.

3. Sauté the onions gently until they begin to soften. For another minute or two, add the spice mix and sauté. Stir in the chickpeas that have been drained and mix well.

4. Make sure the chickpeas are sufficiently heated.

5. Add the greens and sauté until they are just wilted, but they also hold some texture.

8.8. One Pot Quinoa Cannellini Beans Skillet

(Serves 2, Cook Time 35 Minutes, Difficulty: Normal)

Ingredients:

- 2 teaspoons extra-virgin olive oil
- 1 small yellow onion, chopped
- 1 medium red or orange bell pepper, chopped
- 2 cloves garlic, minced
- 1 cup quinoa, uncooked
- 1 teaspoon dried Italian seasoning
- 1/2 teaspoon salt
- 1/4 teaspoon black pepper
- 1 14.5 oz. can diced tomatoes, regular or fire-roasted
- 1 1/2 cups low-sodium vegetable broth
- 1 15.5 oz. can cannellini beans, rinsed and drained
- 3-4 cups fresh spinach or baby spinach

Instructions:

1. Over medium heat, heat the olive oil in a big jar.

Add the onion and bell pepper, and sauté for about 5 minutes until softened.

2. Add the garlic and simmer for another 30 seconds.

3. To boil, add the quinoa, seasonings, tomatoes, and vegetable broth and boil.

4. Cover the kettle, reduce heat to low, and simmer for 15-18 minutes, until the liquid is mostly absorbed and the quinoa is cooked through.

5. Stir in the spinach and cannellini beans until warmed and the spinach is finely wilted, 2-3 minutes.

If needed, serve hot, sprinkled with fresh basil and Parmesan cheese.

8.9. Kung Pao White Beans Skillet

(Serves 2, Cook Time 30 Minutes, Difficulty: Normal)

Ingredients:

- 1/3 cup peanuts
- 3 tbsp. sliced jalapeño pepper (or 3 dried red chilies)
- 1 medium onion, finely chopped
- 2 cloves of garlic, chopped
- 1-inch ginger, finely chopped
- 1/2 tsp. crushed red pepper
- 1/2 red bell pepper
- 1/2 green bell pepper
- 2 15-ounces can white beans, drained and washed

Sauce:

- 1 tbsp. white wine
- 2 tbsp. soy sauce (or tamari)
- 1 tsp. toasted sesame oil
- 2 tbsp. water
- 1 tsp. balsamic vinegar
- 2 tsp. coconut sugar
- 1 tbsp. corn starch

Instructions:

1. Mix the white wine, soy sauce, sesame oil, water, balsamic vinegar, coconut sugar, and cornstarch in a shallow cup.

2. Stir until well mixed and set aside.

3. Heat one tablespoon of oil over medium heat in a big non-stick skillet.

4. Add the peanuts and fry them for about one minute, until they are golden brown.

5. Add the slices of jalapeño pepper, onion, garlic, and ginger.

6. Once the onions are tender, cook for 5-7 minutes and begin to caramelize. Sprinkle with crushed red pepper.

7. Add the red and green bell peppers and roast until the peppers are tender, for another 10 minutes.

8. Add 1/4 cup of water if it sticks to the pan. Stir in the sauce and simmer for 20-30 seconds before the sauce becomes thick and syrupy.

9. To make sure it is covered with the sauce, add the drained white beans and mix.

10. On top of brown rice or as-is, serve sweet.

8.10. Banana & Peanut Butter Quesadillas

(Serves 2, Cook Time 10 Minutes, Difficulty: Normal)

Ingredients:

- 2 bananas
- 2 tbsp. peanut butter
- 2 tortilla wraps
- Cinnamon

Instructions:

1. On low pressure, pop a simple tortilla into a frying pan.

2. Spread the bananas on a generous dollop of peanut butter (about 1-heaped tablespoon) slice.

3. The peanut butter would have begun to melt and go all gooey and yum by the time you have cut them.

4. Sprinkle on the pineapple, accompanied by some cinnamon (about 1 per tortilla).

Fold half of the tortilla and flip it onto a tray.

8.11. Overnight Oats

(Serves 2, Cook Time 5 Minutes, Difficulty: Easy)

(Ready in 5min, Serve 2, Difficulty: Normal)

Ingredients:

- 1 cup porridge oats
- 1 cup of liquid (yoghurt/almond milk/oat milk)
- 1 banana
- 2 tbsp. peanut butter
- Cinnamon

Instructions:

1. In a bowl, mash the banana.

2. Add the liquid cup-we choose yogurt, but instead, you might use almond milk.

3. Stir together, then spoon into cups/jars / whatever you have available.

4. Add the peanut butter + cinnamon and then the oats.

5. For the ingredients to soak up, leave for at least 1 hour.

6. Leave overnight, preferably.

8.12. Porridge

(Serves 2, Cook Time 10 Minutes, Difficulty: Easy)

Ingredients:

- 1 cup porridge oats
- 1 cup of milk

- Toppings such as banana, peanut butter, cinnamon or honey.

Instructions:

1. Over high heat, apply the oats & milk to a plate.

2. Stir until the oats drain all the fluid. Stir in some peanut butter or honey for about 5 minutes.

2. Top with sliced banana & cinnamon spray-Enjoy

8.13. Halloumi Skewers

(Serves 2, Cook Time 20 Minutes, Difficulty: Normal)

Ingredients:

- 225g halloumi
- 2 peppers
- 1 corvette
- 1 red onion
- Skewers - either metal or wooden

Instructions:

1. Cube the Halloumi and chop the red onion, courgette, and peppers into small chunks.

2. Thread the ingredients onto your skewer in any order you wish.

3. Add the skewers to your grill/fire/pan on high heat. Turn regularly and remove once the halloumi is brown and crisp.

8.14. Quesadillas

(Serves 2, Cook Time 15 Minutes, Difficulty: Normal)

Ingredients:

- 1 tin of black beans
- 50g grated cheddar cheese (Approx. 1 handful)

- 50g spring onions
- 1 tsp. cumin
- 1 tsp. lazy chopped chilly (or 1 red chilly chopped)
- 2 tortillas

Instructions:

1. Drain the black beans and add the sliced spring onions, chili, cumin, and cheese to the dish.

2. Using a fork to mash all the ingredients.

3. If needed, add salt and pepper.

Put a frying pan on a medium fire.

4. Using the back of a spoon to add the first tortilla.

5. Spoon to the mashed mixture and spread.

6. Place the second tortilla on top and press down.

7. Cook on either side for 3-4 minutes (until brown / crisp).

8. Flip your quesadilla on a plate and slice it like a pizza.

Chapter 9: Camping Foil Recipes

In this chapter, we will provide you amazing and healthy Foil Recipes that you can cook while camping.

9.1. Camping Breakfast Burritos

(Serves 4, Cook Time 35 Minutes, Difficulty: Normal)

Ingredients:

- 1/2 tablespoon olive oil
- 1 cup frozen hash browns
- 8 oz. cooked ham, diced
- 12 eggs
- 1 tablespoon Old El Paso Taco Seasoning
- 1 (4.5 oz.) can Old El Paso Green Chiles
- 2 cups (8 oz.) shredded cheddar cheese
- 1/4 cup chopped cilantro
- 8 (12-inch) Old El Paso flour tortillas

Instructions:

1. In a large skillet, melt the olive oil. Add the hash browns and cook, stirring continuously, for 1 minute. Continue to cook until the hash browns and ham have both browned, stirring regularly, around 8-10 minutes. Meanwhile, whisk the eggs gently in a wide cup.

In the taco seasoning, whisk.

2. When the hash browns and ham have browned, pour the eggs into the pan. Cook, constantly stirring, until the eggs are ready.

3. Stir in the cilantro, cheese, and green chilies.

4. Tortillas warm up—lower the middle of each tortilla with 1/8 of the egg mixture.

5. Roll up and roll securely in foil like a burrito.

6. In the refrigerator or a freezer, carry in a ziptop container. Place wrapped burritos next to fire in hot coals when ready to cook.

7. Let the burritos remain in the coal, rotating once, about 10-15 minutes until heated through. (How hot the fire is will depend on the time.

9.2. Campfire S'mores Granola

(Serves 4, Cook Time 30 Minutes, Difficulty: Normal)

Ingredients:

The base granola

- 3 cups gluten free rolled oats
- 1/4 cup gluten free oat bran I like it for texture- Can sub for rolled oats
- pinch cinnamon
- pinch sea salt
- 1 T oil of choice or butter
- 1/4 cup pure maple syrup can sub for agave- I didn't try honey for those non vegan

Post grilling/foil baking

- 1 cup + mini marshmallows I used vegan mini marshmallows
- 1 cup + dairy free chocolate chips I used enjoy life mini

Instructions:

1. Generously sprinkle a large sheet of tin foil with oil cooking spray and put it aside to ensure that it is fully coated, including the edges (this makes it easier to open).

2. Combine the oats, oat bran, cinnamon, sea salt and blend well in a large mixing bowl. Add the oil of choice (make sure it's molten if using coconut) and maple syrup and stir until completely added.

3. Put the mixture in the middle portion of the tin foil, ideally in a single sheet, so that there is ample space to wrap around the sides. Wrap the granola up without air space. On the warm stone/coal, lay the foil patch and allow 5-10 minutes to heat.

Shake the foil pack about every 2-3 minutes using tongs to prevent sticking.

4. Detach and open carefully and allow 5 minutes to cool.

5. Generously brush a large sheet of tin foil with oil spray for frying and set aside. Combine the oats, oat bran, cinnamon, sea salt, and blend well in a large mixing cup.

6. Add the oil of choice (make sure it is melted if using coconut) and maple syrup and stir until thoroughly blended. Put the mixture in the middle portion of the tin foil, ideally in a single sheet, so that there is enough space to cover around the sides. Place the tin pouch on medium heat directly on the grill.

7. Remove from the grill and be careful when opening the pouch to giving the granola another stir before allowing it to cool fully.

8. Throw in the marshmallows and chocolate chips.

9. If necessary, stir after 3-4 minutes, or give it a shake (we tried both) and grill the granola for around 10-12 minutes.

9.3. Lumber Jack Break Fast for Camping (in a tin foil)

(Serves 4, Cook Time 15-20 Minutes, Difficulty: Normal)

Ingredients:

- Sausages
- Canadian bacon
- Frozen hash browns,
- leftover cooked potatoes,
- Diced Eggs
- Chopped tomatoes and green onions,
- If you like Shredded cheese, any kind

Instructions:

1. On a double layer of foil that has been lightly coated with cooking spray, lay the sausages or Canadian bacon. To get direct heat from the grill to cook properly, it is better to have the rim's meat.

2. If you don't like beef, cut out the sausages, and start with hash browns and a large dab of butter.

3. Add a couple of frozen hash browns or diced leftover potatoes on top of the sausages, an egg or two, and, if you prefer, a diced tomato and green onion.

4. You may also add Cajun spice, Old Bay spice, or whatever spice your family likes. Wrap up the packet and put it for 15-20 minutes on a hot BBQ or until the meat is thoroughly cooked.

5. BBQ with the cover down to melt the cheese for a few minutes after the packet has cooked for 15-20 minutes.

6. Once the cheese is melted.

9.4. Campfire Orange Cinnamon Rolls

(Serves 4, Cook Time 15 Minutes, Difficulty: Normal)

Ingredients:

- 1 can of 8 cinnamon rolls
- 8 oranges
- Aluminum Foil

Instructions:

1. From the tip, I cut a 2-circle and then used a spoon to scoop the orange out.

We packed the orange flesh with a bowl, and the kids munched on it.

2. Then we just stuck one roll of cinnamon in each orange, put the cap back on, and then wrapped it in foil.

3. We wrapped it from the bottom up so that it was possible to bunch the excess foil into a small handle.

4. We bring it straight into the coals then.

5. It took them about 12 minutes to bake, but your fire depends on that.

6. While they were still piping hot, we put a little drizzle on top of the cinnamon roll of the frosting included in the can.

9.5. Camp Fire Apple Pie Packets

(Serves 4, Cook Time 15 Minutes, Difficulty: Normal)

Ingredients:

- Apple
- Butter
- brown sugar
- ground cinnamon

- dried cranberries or raisins
- chopped pecans or walnuts

Instructions:

1. Preheat the barbecue (to medium heat). Cut a sheet of 12 to 18-inch non-stick foil.

2. Place apple slices together with honey, brown sugar, and butter (on the non-stick side of the foil). (If you use) cinnamon and dried cranberries.

3. Only add a little bit of non-stick spray on the foil if you don't have a non-stick foil to prevent the apples from sticking when baking.

4. With double-fold seals, wrap the packet tightly, leaving a bit of space for heat expansion.

5. Put the packet on the grill and cover, and cook over medium heat for about 15 minutes.

6. Make sure your grate is placed at least 4-6 inches above the charcoals when using a charcoal grill.

7. Use a grill-safe spatula and gently scoop up the packet and place it on a plate. When opening packets, use caution because as you open them, there will be hot steam.

8. Right in the packets, we serve.

9. On the bottom of the packet, there would be juices.

10. In those juices, gently swirl your apples around a little. Eat! And eat!

9.6. Campfire Tex Mix White Bean Chicken Foil Packets

(Serves 4, Cook Time 25 Minutes, Difficulty: Normal)

Ingredients:

- one 15 ounces can navy beans drained and rinsed
- one 10 ounces can diced tomatoes drained
- one 10/11 ounces can mini corn or niblets

- 1 tablespoon Mexican Spice Blend or more to taste!
- 4 boneless skinless chicken breasts diced
- 1/2 cup shredded cheese Mexican blend
- chopped green onion to top
- 4 tin-foil squares about 18" x 12"

Instructions:

1. Combine all the ingredients in a big bowl, except the cheese and the green onion.

On each foil square, put 1/4 of the mixture, fold the tin foil up so the mixture won't leak when turning the packet over the flames.

2. Put over a campfire on a BBQ grill or the rib and cook for 20-25 minutes, sometimes rotating the packets so that everything has been cooked evenly.

3. Once the chicken is thoroughly cooked, remove it from the fire and cool it slightly.

4. On a tray, turn out the foil packets and finish of cheese and green onion.

Enjoy!

9.7. BBQ Party Pack for Campers

(Serves 4, Cook Time 30 Minutes, Difficulty: Normal)

Ingredients:

- 1 cup Red/Orange Bell Peppers, Chopped
- 1 cup Red or White Onion, Chopped
- 1 cup Carrots, 1/2" Square Chop
- 1 cup Russet Potato, 1/2" Square Chop
- 1 cup Zucchini, Chopped
- 1 cup Button or Baby Bella Mushrooms, Chopped
- 1 Cob of Corn, Sliced to 1-2" Wide Medallions

- 2 tablespoons Olive Oil
- 2 teaspoons Liquid Smoke
- 1 1/2 teaspoons Onion Powder
- 1 teaspoon Lemon Juice
- 1 teaspoon Ground Cumin
- 1 teaspoon Smoked Paprika
- 1 teaspoon Chili Powder, Anchor
- 3/4 teaspoon Sea Salt
- 1/2 teaspoon Black Pepper
- 1/2 teaspoon Ground Coriander
- 4- 12 Pieces x8" of Foil, Or just large squares
- Optional: Add pieces of smoked tofu, seitan, chickpeas, etc.

Instructions:

1. Heat up to medium-high heat (around 400oF) on your grill.

2. In a very large bowl, put all the ingredients and toss them together to be well-mixed and evenly coated. Divide the mixture between the four pieces of foil, making each one equivalent to a heaping cup. In the center of the foil, position it.

3. Fold in two sides of the foil toward the middle and fold-down / together until the veggies are reached—flat press. Roll in, towards the middle, take one of the other sides; repeat on the other side until you have a packet. Press the rolls/folds tightly so that they do not quickly fall apart.

4. Put them on the grill and lower the lid, grilling each side of the packet for 8 minutes. You can see if they're ready by peeling back, folding, and testing the corn or potatoes. Open the top of the packets when grilling over the last 4 minutes for a drier mixture inside.

5. Serve warm and, if you like, top with a little more salt and pepper, chili sauce, or BBQ sauce!

9.8. Hobo Dinners

(Serves 4, Cook Time 20-30 Minutes, Difficulty: Normal)

Ingredients:

- 1 lb. Ground beef-I use 93% lean-anything too fatty and your food just sits in a pile of grease
- 1 large potato, scrubbed clean and peeled or not peeled, and sliced thin
- 3 carrots, peeled and cut into sticks
- 1 small onion, cut anyway you want
- Season salt
- Garlic powder
- Pepper
- Butter

Instructions:

1. Divide the ground beef into four equal portions, two slightly larger in our case and two slightly smaller for the kids.

2. Place each of them on their aluminum foil pan. Shake the meat with some seasoned salt and add a little sliced or diced onion.

3. Lay on some potato slices.

4. Sprinkle with some seasoned salt and a little bit of garlic powder.

5. Add the carrot sticks and put the butter on top of a knob or two.

6. Two of the foil's sides are carefully raised and folded over to seal, leaving a pocket of air if necessary.

7. Seal the ends and, over low or medium-low heat or coals, position them on the grill.

8. Close the grill and cook for about 15-20 minutes or until the meat is completely cooked. Alternatively, in a 350-degree oven, bake the meal packages.

9.9. Campfire Paella Foil Packet

(Serves 4, Cook Time 1 Hour, Difficulty: Normal)

Ingredients:

- Raw Mexican chorizo
- Roasted chicken shredded (no skin)
- Onion chopped
- Garlic minced
- Bell pepper chopped
- Cherry tomatoes
- Saffron salt, pepper
- Equal parts uncooked Arborio rice
- Equal parts white wine chicken broth or water

Instructions:

1. Using two non-stick foil sheets to make foil bowls (the dull side in), Fill the bowl with the desired amount of chorizo, chicken, onion, garlic, pepper, tomato, and seasoning.

2. Add rice and wine (or chicken broth or water) in equal quantities. Stir together all. Bring the edges to the top of the foil and close the pouch.

3. Place the open flame next to, but not on, the edge of the campfire.

4. Every 10-15 minutes, rotate it. Cook for one hour or so.

9.10. Campfire Philly Cheesesteak Sandwich

(Serves 4, Cook Time 30 Minutes, Difficulty: Normal)

Ingredients:

- 1 large loaf of French bread
- 1/4 cup garlic butter

- 2 cups cooked, sliced onion and pepper mixture
- 600g sliced roast beef
- 500g provolone cheese, sliced
- Aluminum foil

Instructions:

1. At home, prepare the onion and pepper mixture.

2. Sauté with 1/4 cup of oyster sauce and 2 Tbsp. of butter. Pack to take camping in a container.

4. Start by cutting slices about 1.5 inches apart into the bread and not up to the bottom. The insides of each slice are buttered.

5. Drop into each cut a big scoop of the pepper mixture. Stuff it with cheese and roast beef.

6. Wrap in foil and put until melty and golden near the campfire coals to heat through. Slice the loaf into "sandwich" portions between your 1.5-inch slices from earlier, cutting the bread all the way through.

9.11. BBQ Chicken and Potato Foil Packet

(Serves 4, Cook Time 30 Minutes, Difficulty: Normal)

Ingredients:

- 2 lbs. of boneless skinless chicken tenderloins
- 1 small bag of small golden potatoes
- Your favorite sweet BBQ sauce
- Shredded cheddar cheese
- Olive oil
- Salt
- Pepper

Instructions:

1. With some olive oil, salt, and pepper, cut the potatoes into small pieces and put them evenly in 5 foil packets. The olive oil prevents the potatoes from burning and from sticking to the bottom.

2. Fold the packets up, leaving a little space for steaming at the end, and tightly close the sides. For about 15 minutes, cook the potatoes.

3. To add 2-3 chicken tenderloins and as much BBQ as you want, take the foil packets off the grill and open them. To each package, I normally add a few squirts.

4. Once again, close the packets and cook for an additional 15-25 minutes. Take one off the grill and regularly inspect the chicken.

5. Add a couple of pinches of shredded cheddar cheese to the top when the packets are finished, and serve.

9.12. Easy Pineapple Upside down Cake in Foil Packet
(Serves 4, Cook Time 15 Minutes, Difficulty: Normal)

Ingredients:

- Pineapple chunks, fresh or canned
- Pound cake, cubed {you can also use plain cake donuts, or donut holes}
- Butter
- Brown sugar
- Whipped Cream or ice cream, if desired
- Cinnamon or nutmeg, if desired
- Tin foil
- Cooking Spray

Instructions:

1. Using cooking spray to spray a double layer of tin foil.

2. Attach a couple of slices of pineapple. On top of the pineapple, add pound cake cubes.

3. Apply a healthy dollop of butter and brown sugar to the top of the pineapple and cake.

4. For around 15 minutes, fold up the packet and put on a hot BBQ ... until the butter melts with the brown sugar and forms a sauce at the bottom of the packet over the pineapple.

5. For the last couple of minutes, open the packet to brown the cake a bit.

9.13. Camp Fire Food: Fruit & Sore Cones

(Serves 4, Cook Time 5-7 Minutes, Difficulty: Easy)

Ingredients:

- Chopped Fruit.
- Mini-Marshmallows.
- Chocolate Chips.
- Waffle Ice-Cream Cones...
- Tin Foil.

Instructions:

1. First, our fruit was cut into tiny pieces that became more manageable. We then mixed all our ingredients (fruit, marshmallows, cookies, etc.) in a metal pot.

2. We rolled the cones in foil, and the kids had fun stuffing the waffle cones until they were brimming and bursting! Then we spread the foil over the top and spread it over the fire until the coals had turned ash.

3. Our Fruit and Smote Campfire Cones have been rotated several times.

4. In around 5-7 minutes, they were able to eat!

Chapter 10: Camping Bread Recipes

In this chapter, we will provide you amazing and healthy Bread Recipes that you can cook while camping.

10.1 Zesty Grilled Garlic Bread

(Serves 6, Cook Time 15 Minutes, Difficulty: Normal)

Ingredients:

- ½ cup grated Parmesan cheese
- ½ teaspoon crumbled dried oregano
- ½ teaspoon paprika
- ¼ cup mayonnaise or oil (preferably olive oil) 3 to 4 cloves garlic, minced 1 loaf French bread, sliced lengthwise.

Instructions:

1. Get the barbecue or campfire ready.

2. To bag with the cheese mixture, add mayonnaise and garlic, or blend the ingredients in a small bowl; blend well.

3. Spoon or pour a variation of mayonnaise over the two halves of the sliced bread.

4. Place bread on the grill, sliced side up if the grill is available; otherwise, place bread

halves together, top sides facing each other, and cover in foil.

5. Place it for 5 to 10 minutes over the medium sun, turning regularly.

10.2. Bread-On-A-Stick

(Serves 2, Cook Time 15 Minutes, Difficulty: Normal)

Ingredients:

- 1 cup all-purpose flour
- 1 teaspoon baking powder
- ¼ teaspoon salt
- 1 cup cold water All-purpose flour for shaping dough (approx. ¼ cup) Butter and/or jam for serving

Instructions:

1. Get the barbecue or campfire ready.

2. Peel the green sticks at the top to extract the bark.

3. Combine the flour mixture and water in a mixing bowl; blend easily.

4. Before they form a hard dough. (If you do not have a convenient cup, you should apply the water with the flour mixture to the bag and knead it right in the bag.)

5. Flatten the dough into 1 or 2 patties around 1/2 inch thick with floured hands.

6. Wrap a green stick around the end and hold it over the hot coals.

7. Turn until cooked through, repeatedly. Slide off with butter and jam and serve hot.

10.3. Warm Wild Berry Jam

(Serves 2, Cook Time 15 Minutes, Difficulty: Normal)

Ingredients:

- 4 cups wild berries (blueberries, strawberries, blackberries, or a mixture)
- 3 cups sugar

- One-quarter of a lemon

Instructions:

1. In a medium pot, combine the berries and sugar.

2. Put over high-medium heat. Stir to blend the sugar and the berries, and then let it be. Heat the boiling mixture.

4. Squeeze in the mixture of lemon juice and stir rapidly.

5. Remove from the heat to cool and set aside.

10.4. Corn Tortillas

(Serves 4, Cook Time 1 Hours, Difficulty: Normal)

Ingredients:

- 2 cups masa harina* (corn flour; available in large supermarkets or Mexican markets)
- ½ teaspoon salt
- 2 cups boiling water You will also need: Waxed paper or tortilla press

Instructions:

1. In a medium dish, stir all together naan and salt. Make a well in the center and add about half a cup of boiling water.

2. Shake well, then add water a little at a time, first stirring with a spoon and then adding with the hands until the mixture is well blended (once the water has cooled enough).

3. It wants to be firm and springy rather than dry and crumbly. Cover and leave to stand for around 1 hour. Heat a skillet or griddle over medium-high heat.

4. Break the dough into two-inch balls.

5. Roll out a ball between two wet waxed paper pieces (a bottle of wine or a can of vegetables works well as a rolling pin) or flatten it with a tortilla press; the tortillas should be very thin and even.

6. Peel off one sheet of waxed paper gently and put the tortilla, paper side up, on a hot

skillet. Peel off another sheet of waxed paper as the tortilla heats up. If the first side is golden brown, turn the tortilla and cook until the second side is golden brown.

7. Hold your towel warm when cooking the remaining tortillas.

10.5. Cheddar Biscuit

(Serves 4, Cook Time 30-60 Minutes, Difficulty: Normal)

Ingredients:

- 2½ cups all-purpose flour
- 1½ teaspoons baking powder
- ½ teaspoon baking soda
- ½ teaspoon salt
- 5 tablespoons unsalted butter, cut into ½-inch pieces
- 1 cup shredded cheddar cheese
- 1 cup buttermilk or plain yogurt
- 1 egg

Instructions:

1. Heat the oven to 450 degrees F. Mix the flour mixture and unsalted butter together in a mixing dish.

2. Break the butter into the flour with 2 -knives until the paste is crumbly. Stir in the cheese that has been shredded. In a different cup, beat buttermilk and egg until frothy together.

3. Stir the buttermilk mixture into the flour mixture with a wooden spoon to form a lumpy dough.

4. Flour the work surface gently and turn the dough out on it. Gently knead about 10-times and then stretch the dough out to a thickness of a little less than 1/2 inch.

5. Break the dough into 2-inch squares with a clean, sharp knife and put it on an ungreased baking dish.

10.6. Skillet Bread

(Serves 4-6, Cook Time 15 Minutes, Difficulty: Normal)

Ingredients:

- ¼ cup vegetable oil or shortening
- 2¼ cups buttermilk baking mix, divided
- 2¼ cups buttermilk baking mix, divided
- ½ cup cold water
- 4 wild scallions, chopped

Instructions:

1. Make sure your cooking fire, whether it's a campfire or a grill, has a steady, low flame—heat oil or melt shortening in a skillet with at least an 8-inch-wide rim.

2. Stir 2 cups of the baking mix, the water, and the scallions together in the mixing bowl until the mixture is well combined.

3. With the leftover baking mix, coat your hands, then pat the dough into a softball. Place the dough in the saucepan and flatten it, taking care not to burn your hands.

4. Cook the bread until the bottom begins to brown, and it starts to dry out. Take caution not to let the flames get too hot, or it would ruin the bread.

5. When the first side is nicely browned, flip and cook the bread until the second side is browned and the middle is no longer doughy.

Chapter 11: Camping Sea Food Recipes

In this chapter, we will be presenting fish and sea food recipes for campers.

11.1. Lime-Drizzled Fish Tacos

(Serves 8, Cook Time 25 Minutes, Difficulty: Normal)

Ingredients:

- 4 Tilapia fish filets
- ¼ cup chipotle dressing
- 1 cup cilantro, chopped
- 2 tomatoes, diced
- 1 red onion, diced
- 2 limes, juiced
- 8 tacos Vegetable oil Marinade
- 3 tablespoons honey
- 1 teaspoon cumin
- 1 teaspoon oregano
- 1 teaspoon cayenne pepper

- 1 lime, juiced
- ¼ cup extra virgin olive oil

Instructions:

1. Mix the marinade ingredients.

2. With the marinade, put the tilapia in a dish and allow the fish to marinate for an hour.

3. Bring the fire to moderate and fill the grid with just a little vegetable oil.

4. Barbecue until the fish is flakey for 8 minutes to ensure the tilapia is about 5 inches from the fire.

5. On the barbecue, heat the tacos for a minute.

6. Cover with coriander tacos, peas, chipotle sauce, red onions, flake tuna, drizzle with lime juice, and slice between tacos

11.2. Orange Bacon Salmon Skewers

(Serves 4, Cook Time 15 Minutes, Difficulty: Normal)

Ingredients:

- 1 pound salmon filets
- 2 oranges, segmented
- 8 bacon slices

Instructions:

1. Chop 1-inch-bits of salmon

2. Position the salmon with orange segments on the skewers.

3. Wrap them with 2-slices of bacon per skewer.

4. When keeping it 6 inches above the fire and 6 inches over the fire, cook salmon over a fire.

5. Cook for about 7 minutes.

11.3. Grilled Shrimp and Mushrooms

(Serves 4, Cook Time 10 Minutes, Difficulty: Normal)

Ingredients:

- 1½ pounds jumbo shrimp, shelled and deveined
- 12 Cri mini mushrooms 8 garlic cloves, finely-chopped
- 1 lemon, juiced
- ½ teaspoon paprika
- ½ teaspoon salt
- ½ teaspoon black pepper
- ¼ teaspoon extra virgin olive oil
- Vegetable oil

Instructions:

1. For extra virgin olive oil, mix the cinnamon, black pepper, paprika, lemon juice, and garlic.

2. For the marinade, marinate the shrimp and mushrooms for an hour.

3. On skewers, string mushrooms, and shrimp.

4. To spray your grill and heat up to medium, use a little vegetable oil.

5. For around 6 minutes, cook the mushroom shrimp skewers and serve them with a salad.

11.4. Ying and Yang Salmon

(Serves 4, Cook Time 10 Minutes, Difficulty: Normal)

Ingredients:

- 6-ounce wild salmon steaks
- 2 teaspoon Mirin
- 1 lemon, juiced

- 4 tablespoons soy sauce
- ¼ cup honey Vegetable Oil

Instructions:

1. Combine the mirin, lemon juice, honey, and soy sauce.

2. Put the marinade on the salmon steaks.

3. Enable it for an hour to marinate.

4. Heat your grill to high, and grease the grates loosely.

5. Brush the honey with the salmon and put it on the grill.

6. Cook for 10 minutes, turning over as the fish releases itself from the grater happily. After 5 minutes, this could occur. 7. Serve the fish with grilled vegetables and rice.

11.5. Tequila Jalapeño Scallops

(Serves 4, Cook Time 15 Minutes, Difficulty: Normal)

Ingredients:

- 1½ pounds scallops
- ¼ cup tequila
- 1 lime, juiced
- 2 jalapeños, sliced
- 1 teaspoon salt
- 1 teaspoon black pepper
- Vegetable oil

Instructions:

1. Mix the tequila, lime juice, salt, black pepper, and jalapeños and marinate with the scallops for 15 minutes.

2. 3 scallops per skewer, position.

3. Heat a medium-high grill and apply vegetable oil to the spray.

4. Place skewers so that on the grill, the scallops are flat out.

5. Grill each side for 2 minutes.

6. Serve with a tequila shot and pasta!

11.6. Grilled Snapper

(Serves 4, Cook Time 8 Minutes, Difficulty: Normal)

Ingredients:

- 4 red snapper fish
- 1 lemon, sliced 1-2 lemons, juiced
- Salt and pepper
- Extra virgin olive oil

Instructions:

1. Grab 4-sticks or skewers for roasting.

2. Brush each fish with a little extra virgin olive oil, sprinkle with salt and pepper, and stick a lemon slice on either side of the fish. Bring the skewer through the fish.

3. Keep the fish 6 inches above the fire, and simmer for 8 minutes or so.

4. Drizzle, if needed, with salt and lemon juice. Enjoy!

Conclusion

There are also many other types of campfires available, and they have definite explanations of their own. Nonetheless, like every form of outdoor design, layout and upkeep takes a tremendous amount of work to make it flawless. We see why a mother always tells her kids not to play with flame. As it is so strong that it can save and demolish, you can treat it with esteem. Please remember that protection precautions should be taken until the use of the fire has been done. Cover the fire with water, and even cover it with soil and dust if there are any leftovers from the campfire. If you do not pay attention to the burning, so the assets will be badly affected. Consequently, always take precautions so that everything cannot be lost.

Printed in Great Britain
by Amazon